M000079329

ESTHER HAUTZIG

Life With Working Parents

PRACTICAL HINTS FOR EVERYDAY SITUATIONS

Illustrated by ROY DOTY

MACMILLAN PUBLISHING CO., INC.
New York
COLLIER MACMILLAN PUBLISHERS
London

FOR WALTER HAUTZIG
AND OUR CHILDREN

Special thanks to our son David for his helpful and
sharp-eyed advice while I was working on this book.

Macmillan Publishing Co., Inc.
866 Third Avenue, New York, N.Y. 10022
Collier Macmillan Canada, Ltd.
Printed in the United States of America

10 9 8 7 6 5 4 3 2 1

LIBRARY OF CONGRESS CATALOGING IN PUBLICATION DATA
Hautzig, Esther Rudomin.   Life with working parents.
Bibliography: p.   Includes index.   SUMMARY: A guide for children
who must cope with a variety of daily situations on their own because
their parents work.   1. Children of working mothers—Juvenile literature.
2. Home economics—Juvenile literature.   3. Cookery—Juvenile
literature.   4. Handicraft—Juvenile literature.   [1. Children of working
mothers.   2. Home economics.   3. Cookery.   4. Handicraft]
I. Doty, Roy, date   II. Title.   III. Title: Working parents.
HQ777.6.H35   649'.1   76-15223   ISBN 0-02-743500-8

Contents

Introduction

This book is intended for boys and girls whose mother and father both work and for those living with a single parent who has a full-time job. It may also prove useful to young people whose parents have part-time jobs, or for those whose parents go to school or to college, or even, at times, for those whose parent is ill and not able to be in charge of the household.

Whenever there is no one in the family spending full time at housekeeping, everyone must pitch in to take care of things. There is much that you can do to help your mother and/or your father to cope with a full working day, a home and a family. Every boy and girl whose parents work can become a capable, responsible member of the family team. And when household chores are shared by all, there is always more time for the whole family to spend together in a relaxed and calm way, doing things everyone enjoys. With a little organization, cooperation and good will, life with parents who have full-time jobs need not be chaotic, rushed or harassed.

You can also feel happier with the time you spend at home alone if you've planned for it. It can be rather nice to have the house all to yourself! You can sit and daydream, work at hobbies, read, watch whatever you like on TV without any flack from grownups, have a snack while the radio or phonograph plays full blast, do chores and whatever else you like without any interference.

Being on your own and handling things by yourself will make you feel tremendously self-reliant and independent—and good about yourself. Helping to run your household will also prepare you for the day when you will be living on your own.

The various sections in this book provide hints on such things as organizing working schedules, knowing safety measures, preparing simple meals and helping to keep things neat at home, using appliances, taking care of pets, baby-sitting with younger brothers and sisters, as well as on having fun during your free times. There is advice on coping if your parents work at home, or if one of them travels a lot or lives away from you. You will find recipes, projects and book lists, plant-tending pointers and all sorts of other useful things.

The chief purpose of this book, however, is to help *you* learn to cope on your own in your own way, and to work out with your mom and/or dad a routine that is happy, comfortable and efficient. Each family must discuss carefully its own situation, working schedules, wants and needs, and do so with warm and loving consideration for each other's likes and dislikes and innermost feelings. Whenever possible, divide the tasks according to everyone's special capabilities and preferences. You may enjoy preparing meals for an entire week, while your mother may hate to cook and be just as happy to paint the living room. Your father may

love to tend the plants in your home and do the vacuuming, while your sister would rather be in complete
charge of caring for the family's pets or mowing the
lawn.

There will be frequent times, of course, when each
member of the family will have to do things that he or
she dislikes or does not know much about. I hope that
the advice and hints included in this book will show
you how to cope at such times, and also help you find
great enjoyment in your independence and sense of accomplishment. Along with work well done, I hope that
you will have many happy times and fulfilling experiences with everyone in the family, doing things you
all like to do.

1 · General Suggestions and Hints

One of the most important things to do when both of your parents work—or when you live with a single parent who has a full-time job—is to discuss household priorities and organize plans. Discuss what is important to the various members of your family in the daily running of your home—neat rooms, well-planned meals, laundry folded and put away or whatever. With the various family priorities in mind, make a list with your parents of what can be taken care of by each member of the family. Everyone should take turns doing such things as fixing breakfasts and box lunches, doing dishes, starting supper, doing laundry, etc. Be sure you know what your parents expect of you, and that in your family work as well as pleasures are shared by all in an equal and fair way.

Ask to visit the places where your parents work. It is nice to know what the store or office or factory looks like and where your mom or dad sits or stands at work. It is also fun to meet the people with whom your parents work all day. Later, when your mother or father mentions a name, you will know who is meant. Ask questions and talk to your mom and dad about their jobs—the way they ask you questions about your school work, your friends, your activities. The more you know about your parents' jobs—what they do, where they do it and how their work affects other people—the easier it will be to cope with their absences from home. Life can be much more exciting if *everyone* in the family shares news of his or her doings —at school, at home and at work.

Try not to overwhelm your parents with complaints, arguments and problems the minute they come home from their jobs. It is important to tell them what is worrying you, or what made you furious with your brother or sister or friend. Just try not to do it the minute they step through the door. Your mother and father need a few minutes to catch their breath. After that, they can enjoy even more being with you and hearing all about your day.

Discuss with your parents how you should spend your alone-at-home time, so that everyone, but most especially you, feels comfortable and at ease about the situation. Allow free time for after-school activities such as music lessons, sports or clubs. Mark your calendar or the family calendar so that you will know what *you* are to do, and when, on each day of the week.

If you are an only child, or have no sisters or brothers old enough to share responsibilities, do one big task assigned to you each day. Since none of us is a computer—and even computers have their off-days —there may be times when you cannot do the tasks agreed upon. If too many days like this come up and you begin to feel pressured and unhappy, reevaluate your schedule with your family. Is the work really fairly distributed among all the members of the family? Possibly you have too much to do. Talk it over calmly and frankly. It is much better to discuss things than to be resentful and unhappy and to perform your tasks grudgingly and therefore badly.

DOING HOMEWORK will undoubtedly be at the top of your after-school schedule. No matter how many projects or chores you may have on your afternoon schedule, your·mom or dad will want to be sure your homework gets done. Discuss with them how you and they would like to see it handled. Maybe they will want you to do your homework when one of them is at home. Possibly they will think it's better for you to do most of your homework while they are still at work. If you find you need help with something, you can finish it after your parents have returned. At any rate, decide what your homework schedule should be and try to stick to it every day.

IF YOU GO TO VISIT A FRIEND and have not told your parents or a sister or brother that you were going to do so, call one of them and tell them where you are and when you expect to come home. If your parents do not want you to walk home alone after dark, leave while it is still light or make arrangements to be picked up by someone. Possibly your friend's parent or older brother or sister will be able to see you home. In any case, be sure that arrangements are made and that your parents know what is happening.

IF YOU BRING A FRIEND HOME, here are a few things you might bear in mind. Does your friend's mother or father know that you two are at your home? If not, be sure to call your friend's house and tell whoever is there that you are in your home by yourselves. Also be sure your mother or father knows that you have brought a friend to your house. Telephone them if you haven't discussed it before.

Try to play quiet games with your friend. Real roughhousing can lead to all sorts of trouble—broken chairs, bloody noses, even broken bones. Play Scrabble, or Monopoly, or chess or checkers or whatever games you have and like. Just talking with a friend in a quiet house can be one of the most pleasant ways of passing time. It is seldom possible in some households—with other people around and televisions, radios or phonographs playing—to have a quiet talk with a friend about anything and everything. If you have a task for that afternoon, maybe your friend can help you. The next time you can help your friend.

If you can't think of anything to do with a friend on a quiet afternoon, here are a few simple projects, with directions, for you to explore.

Three-Dimensional Pictures

You will need: newspapers; one piece of construction paper or cardboard; macaroni or beans of different shapes; glue; pencil.

Do it this way:
1. Cover your working area with newspapers. Glue

macaroni or beans on the construction paper or cardboard in any kind of design that you and your friend may choose.

2. You can make a design of your family initials. Write them first with a pencil and then glue macaroni or beans over the letters in an interesting pattern.

3. Do not pick up the paper or cardboard with the design on it until the glue has dried completely. If you pick it up too soon, the beans and macaroni may fall off.

Make Music on a Comb (or other "instrument")

You will need: two combs; toilet paper.

Do it this way:
1. Put a piece of toilet paper over each comb.
2. Each of you hum, with mouth held slightly open, into a comb. The noises the combs make are fun to hear and to harmonize with.

You can also use two empty cans (be sure they do not have rough edges) to bang together. One of you can play on the comb-and-paper "harmonica" while the other crashes "cymbals" made of two cans.

Write a Joint Poem or Story

You will need: two pencils or pens; several sheets of paper.

Do it this way:
1. Think of a subject or a theme—serious or funny.

2. One of you write the first line of a poem or first sentence of a story; then the other write the second. Continue in turn until the story or poem is finished.
3. Be sure that you both write each other's, as well as your own, sentences on your own sheets of paper. When you are done, each of you will have a jointly created original tale or poem to keep for yourself or to share with your family.

Make Picture Puzzles

You will need: two full-page pictures from a magazine; two pieces of cardboard; glue; scissors; pencil.

Do it this way:
1. Glue a picture to each piece of cardboard.
2. On the back of one cardboard have your friend draw shapes of whatever kind and size he or she wishes. You do the same with the other cardboard.
3. Cut the cardboards into pieces along the lines drawn. Put each of the puzzles in separate piles.
4. Let your friend assemble the puzzle you have cut, and you assemble the one your friend has made.

IF YOU HAVE ABSOLUTELY NOTHING TO DO. When you live with working parents, times with absolutely nothing to do aren't all that frequent—there are always things to be done around the house or yard or kitchen. But for those afternoons when there is really nothing else for you to do but watch TV and feel sorry for yourself, you might take out craft books from your library. A short list of such books is given at the end of this book. If you do not have any such books at home and you are about to go out of your skull from boredom, here are just a few suggestions for things to make and do.

Start a Personal Diary.

You will need: notebook from the dime store; decorative paper; glue; label; felt-tip pen; scissors.

Do it this way:
1. Decorate the notebook by pasting pretty paper over its covers. Paste a label on the front cover and with bold letters write on it "Personal Diary, Do Not Open."
2. You needn't write in your diary every day. When you feel like it or on a day when you have little to do, you can write about things that mean a lot to you, or things that have happened, or things you want to do in the future.

Sort and File Your Important Sports Cards.

You will need: empty shoe or cigar boxes; decorative paper; glue; scissors.

Do it this way:
1. Decorate the shoe boxes or cigar boxes by pasting attractive paper all over the boxes and their covers.
2. Paste a baseball card on top of the box in which you will file your baseball cards, a hockey card on top of the box in which you will file your hockey cards, etc.

3. Sort out all your cards and file them away in the appropriate boxes. You can also file school papers, clippings from magazines and letters from friends in such box files. If you do this, and store the boxes on your shelves, you will not need to search for your important belongings when you need them.

Make a Folder for Keeping Coupons, Cleaner's Receipts, etc.

You will need: notebook from the dime store; decorative paper; glue; pencil or felt-tip pen; scissors.

Do it this way:
1. Glue the first two pages of the notebook together on two of the open sides. Leave one side open. Repeat, two pages at a time, throughout the whole notebook. These glued-together pages will form "envelopes" for keeping coupons, receipts, etc.
2. With felt-tip pen or a pencil, write on each of these "envelopes" what you intend to keep in them— coupons, receipts, etc.
3. Decorate the cover with colorful paper.

Make a Family Mailbox

You will need: small empty detergent box; label; pencil or felt-tip pen; single-edge razor blade; sharp scissors; decorative paper; glue; nail and hammer.

Do it this way:
1. Clean the detergent box by shaking it so that all remaining detergent comes out.

2. With the razor blade or scissors, cut off the top part of the box.

3. Glue decorative paper all over the box. Write "Family Mail" on the label and glue it in the center of the box.

4. Using a nail and hammer, punch a small hole on one of the wide sides (not the one that has the label) of the box. Then, if your parents permit it, put a nail in your wall and hang up the decorated mailbox. If you cannot put a nail in your wall for this purpose, let the mailbox stand on a shelf or counter.

Make a Telephone Message Box

You will need: empty kitchen matchbox, or another box of similar or slightly larger size; decorative paper; scissors; glue; felt-tip pen; string; pencil; masking tape.

Do it this way:

1. Glue decorative paper all over the box.

2. On top of the box write "Telephone Messages," using a colorful felt-tip pen.

3. Cut a piece of string, twine or wool, about 15 inches long.

4. Using colorful masking tape, attach one end of the string to a pencil, and the other end of the string to the message box. Put a small pad of paper inside the box. Keep this box near your telephone so that messages can be written down and kept in one place.

2 · Safety Rules and Measures

The advice in this section is given not to frighten you, but to help you deal with different situations. Such situations occur most often in large cities, but they can come up on suburban streets and in small towns as well. Wherever you live, if trouble occurs, remember to keep your cool, not to panic and to follow safety directions given to you by your parents. The words in this chapter may prove useful as well.

KEEP A FEW DIMES IN YOUR POCKET for making calls from a public telephone booth. It is important to have a dime or two in case you have to get in touch with one of your parents or a neighbor while you are out, or if your home telephone does not work.

KNOW THE LOCATION OF THE POLICE ALARM BOX AND THE FIRE ALARM BOX in your neighborhood. If you are in trouble outside and all the public phone booths are broken, it is good to know where these boxes are located.

TAKE A BUS WHENEVER POSSIBLE if you live in a large city and it is too far to walk to the dentist, the barbershop, the library or wherever. The driver in a bus can be counted on for help if help is needed. If you must take a subway, get into the first car of the train (where the conductor is), or one in which you see a lot of people. While waiting for the train, stand with other people, not in the deserted parts of the subway station platform. There is safety in numbers.

PAY ATTENTION TO TRAFFIC. Never cross a city street on a red light, even if you do not see any oncoming cars. A driver in a parked car may suddenly take off. Do not cross in the middle of the block, even if the street seems clear of traffic.

Do not dash into a street from in between parked cars to retrieve a ball or Frisbee or other toy you may have been tossing around. Wait until the ball rolls back to the curb—it almost always does—and then pick it up. Ask for a grownup's assistance if your toy is hopelessly "marooned" in the middle of the street. Do not go into traffic by yourself.

When you cross a street or road where there is no traffic light, stop and look carefully in both directions. Make sure that there is no oncoming traffic from either side. Don't dash onto the road from in front or in back of a school bus. Obey all traffic rules in your area. They are designed to protect you.

Even if you do not see or hear a train, never cross railroad tracks on foot or on a bicycle if there is a red light or a lowered railroad crossing bar. Wait until the railroad traffic light turns green and/or the crossing bars go up.

STAY OUT OF UNKNOWN NEIGHBORHOODS, especially after dark. Walk on familiar streets and take well-known routes. Never take short cuts through deserted lots, tunnels or abandoned buildings.

NEVER ACCEPT OFFERS OF CANDY OR OTHER TREATS OR RIDES FROM STRANGERS. No matter how nice the person may be to you, never accept a thing from anyone you do not know well. Never eat anything offered to you, never accept a treat from anyone you do not know and never, ever get into a stranger's car.

IF YOU ARE FOLLOWED ON THE STREET AND YOU ARE FRIGHTENED, cross the street or change the direction in which you are walking. If you are still being followed, run and scream as loudly as you can. Try to attract someone's attention, and don't worry if you look foolish.

IF YOU ARE ATTACKED ON THE STREET and someone takes away your money and possibly your keys and other possessions, do the following:
1. Give up what your attackers want without an argument; it's better than being hurt.
2. As soon as your attackers are out of reach and cannot hit you or hurt you, start yelling as loudly as you can. Stomp your feet, flail your arms, raise the biggest rumpus you can. Not only does it alert the people near you to what has happened, but it also helps to relieve your tension and fright.
3. If you have not alerted a nearby policeman with your shrieks, look for one as quickly as you can. If you

do not see one on the street, call from a police box or from a public telephone booth. Policemen are kind and helpful people and you should tell them what happened. Try to describe to them what your attackers looked like, what they wore and anything unusual which you may have noticed.

4. The police may want to take you to look for your attackers in the immediate neighborhood where the trouble took place. If your carfare or bus pass has been stolen, the police will make arrangements to see that you get home safely.

5. If your keys were also stolen, along with a bus pass which had your name on it or some other identification paper, go to a neighbor's house, not to your own home. Call your parents and tell them what happened. One of your parents will deal with the situation from then on, as the locks in your home may have to be changed.

6. Discuss what happened to you with your parents. Being attacked is frightening, and talking about it afterward helps.

IF YOU HAVE A BICYCLE, observe these safety precautions. Do not ride a bicycle on a city sidewalk. You can run into people, especially little kids. When you ride a bicycle on the street, observe all traffic rules. Ride with traffic, on the right side of the street or road. Be particularly careful at intersections and watch out for opening car doors, potholes, soft shoulders, drains, etc. Use hand signals if you turn or stop. If you don't know the hand signals, ask one of your parents to teach them

to you. Be sure that your bike has front, rear and pedal reflectors, a bell and good brakes.

To prevent theft, never leave your bicycle unattended and unchained. If you must leave your bike for a little while, chain it to some permanently attached object with a heavy-duty chain and a good padlock. Pull the chain through both wheels and bike frame and then lock it up. Do not leave a bicycle outside overnight.

If you go bike-riding in city parks, do not go alone if possible. Go with a friend or two. Avoid out-of-the-way park paths or heavily wooded or hilly areas. Ride where there are lots of people. If you notice a threatening group of kids holding sticks or other objects with which you could be hit, make a quick get-away or approach an adult for protection. Of course, if you are threatened and ordered to hand over your bicycle, do so without argument and follow the advice in the previous section.

IF YOU WALK HOME ALONE on a city street, don't swing your keys so that everyone can see that you may be letting yourself into your home by yourself. Don't show that you are carrying money. Keep your money and your keys in your pants or coat pocket.

If you live in an apartment house and a stranger follows you into your building and into the elevator, and you feel uneasy for any reason, get off on the next floor. Walk or take another elevator back to your building lobby and wait there or in the street until you see someone you know come into your building. Ask the person you know to go up with you to your floor and to wait until you have let yourself into your apartment. You can also ring a friendly neighbor's doorbell in such a situation and ask for help.

If you live in the suburbs and a stranger follows you into your driveway, do not unlock your door. Go to your closest neighbor's house and explain the situation to them.

IF YOU COME HOME ALONE and see that your door has been tampered with, or if it is unlocked, or if you see a broken lock or broken window or anything else the least bit suspicious, do not go into your apartment or house. Go to a neighbor's house, to your superintendent's apartment if it is in your building or to a public telephone on the street and call your parents. Tell them what you saw and tell them where you are. Stay away from your apartment or house until one of your parents comes, or until a neighbor or grown-up friend goes in and checks to see that all is well.

LEAVE A SET OF KEYS to your home with a close neighbor or friend. In case you have been locked out of your home by accident, or have lost your keys, you will be able to get in if there is an extra set of keys with a friend or neighbor. If you live in the suburbs or in the country, you can put an extra set of keys in the unlikeliest of hiding places—a place no burglar or intruder would think of investigating. Never put a set of keys under the doormat, in your mailbox, milk box or anywhere else obvious.

NEVER LEAVE YOUR DOOR UNLOCKED, not even if you go out for just a minute to walk the dog or to mail a letter or to visit your next-door neighbor. It does not take an intruder long to get into your home. When you go out, always lock the door and take your keys with you.

IF YOU GET LOCKED OUT OF YOUR HOME and none of your neighbors or friends has a spare set of keys to your home, telephone your parents from a neighbor's or friend's house to let them know what happened. If it is close to their coming-home time, just sit down in front of your door and try to think pleasant thoughts, or stay with the friend or neighbor until one of your parents returns. Be sure to tell your parents if by some chance you have left something cooking in the oven or on the stove. In that case one of your parents may be able to leave work and come home sooner.

IF SOMEONE RINGS THE DOORBELL when you are home alone, never open the door without asking who it is and looking through the peephole if your door has one. If you recognize the name *and* voice of the doorbell ringer, or his or her face—it may be a neighbor or an unexpected relative or friend—open the door.

If you do not recognize the person who is ringing your doorbell, never open your door under any circumstances, even if the person says that he or she has come to read your electric or gas meter, make a delivery, give you a message from your parents, spray for roaches or whatever. Say that you would like him or her to come back later, and give a specific time when you know that one of your parents will be home. Do not say that you are home alone. You can do all this, of course, in as polite a manner as you know how, but don't sacrifice safety for politeness. It is better to be rude than to put yourself into what might be a dangerous situation. If the person doesn't go away and keeps ringing or knocking, call the police.

If the person says that he or she needs to use the telephone for an emergency, offer to make the call for that person, but never, ever let anyone you do not know into your home.

WHEN YOU ANSWER THE TELEPHONE, do the following: When the telephone rings, say "hello." The telephone company advises against answering the phone by saying "Smiths' residence" or "This is Adam Smith" or "Melissa Smith" or whatever your name may be. There is no reason to identify yourself by name until you know who is calling. If you do not know the caller, don't say that you are at home alone, don't give out family information or your address. If the caller wants to speak to one of your parents, tell him or her that your parent is unable to speak right now but will call back later. Get the name of the person who is calling, his or her telephone number and the message. Write down everything slowly and carefully. Put the message in a previously agreed upon place for messages, such as your family bulletin board or a specially made box for messages (see page 13).

Always have a pen or pencil and a small pad by the telephone. If you have more than one telephone, have a pen or pencil and a pad by each.

If you get a crank call—someone saying silly or nasty things to you—hang up immediately. Do not get into any kind of conversation. A person who makes such calls wants to keep you talking and listening to him or her. The sooner you hang up, the better it will be for everyone involved. Report such calls to your parents; if you get many of them, your parents surely will report them to your local telephone company.

KEEP TELEPHONE NUMBERS of relatives, close neighbors or friends who are usually at home by your telephone, on your bulletin board or in another prominent place in your home. It will make you feel more comfortable, and your parents too, to know that in an emergency you can reach others in addition to your mom or dad. Also have your parents' business numbers and the numbers of the doctor, fire department and police department by each telephone in your home and on your bulletin board. It is not a bad idea to add the number of the nearest poison control center to the list. There are over six hundred of these centers around the country, and they will give you advice over the telephone if you or anyone in the family accidentally swallows something poisonous.

HAVE WORKING FLASHLIGHTS in your home and be sure to keep them always in the same places. In case of power failure, you will be able to get around your home with a flashlight until the electricity goes on again. A good place for one flashlight is a night table or other place near your bed.

DO NOT TAKE A BATH OR SHOWER IF YOU ARE ALL ALONE AT HOME, unless absolutely necessary. Bathrooms can be slippery at times. If you fall and hurt yourself and cannot get to the telephone, there will be no one to help you. It is also a good idea not to lock a bathroom door whenever you take a bath or shower. Why not make a sign saying "Occupied" on one side and "Free" on the other, and put it on the bathroom door? The worst accidents at home can and do happen in the bathroom. If you fall and hurt yourself, it is easier for someone to get to you if the bathroom door stays unlocked.

IF YOU DON'T FEEL WELL when you are alone at home, never take any medicines without first checking with one of your parents.

If your mom or dad tells you to take an aspirin or some other mild medication, do so. Be sure you read the labels on your medicine bottles carefully and that you take exactly what you were told to take. Lie down for an hour or so—or until someone comes home. If the ache or pain gets worse, call your parent again and report. He or she will know what to do—whether to call your doctor, dentist or whomever. If you feel so uncomfortable that you do not want to be at home by yourself, tell your parent that on the telephone. Perhaps you will be allowed to go over to a neighbor's or some nearby friend's house to wait for someone to come and get you.

KNOW FIRE PREVENTION MEASURES AND WHAT TO DO IN CASE OF FIRE. The fire department in your community probably has booklets that give information and advice on how to prevent fires and how to act in case a fire has broken out. Write to your fire department and ask for their free booklets on this subject. In the meantime, here are some directions based on information supplied by a large city fire department.

Have a Regular Family Fire Drill

1. Carefully plan with your mom and dad escape routes from each room in your home in case of fire. Alternate routes should also be decided on, in case the normal route is blocked by fire.

2. Make sure that each member of the family can open all doors and windows in your home.

3. Memorize the number in your community for reporting a fire. In case the telephone does not work, each one in the family should know where the nearest fire alarm box is located. The person who discovers a fire should turn in the alarm immediately and alert the whole family to the danger.

4. If possible, each bedroom should have a flashlight to assist in escape. The whole family should know where to meet after they have left the house. Choose a well-lighted street corner. This will help to make sure that every member of the family has escaped safely.

How to Escape From a Fire

1. Do not panic. Walk quickly to the nearest exit. If it is blocked, use the alternate route which your family has agreed upon.

2. Feel the door. If the door is hot, do not open it. There may be flames on the other side, and a draft can spread the fire.

3. To travel through heavy smoke, keep close to the floor. The air is cooler near the floor.

4. In an apartment building use stairs, not an elevator. The elevator may trap you.

5. Do not go back for any of your things. Things can always be replaced; people can't.

6. If trapped inside a room, open a window from the bottom for fresh air and from the top to let heat and smoke out. Stay calm and wait for someone to come for you.

3 · Helping With Housework

Keeping a home neat does not really require a great deal of work. Keeping a house scrupulously clean does, but that is not your job! Whatever you do to help, though, will make life easier for the whole family. It will give your mom and dad more time to do fun things with you when they are home. It will also give you a great sense of accomplishment—and be very helpful in years to come when you are on your own. Discuss with your parents how you can help.

The first thing you will have to do, no doubt, is keep your own—or shared—room picked up and reasonably neat. (Keep your door closed if your room is in ruins!) Make your bed before you leave for school or right after you come home. Put away toys, books, records and other things so that they do not clutter up your room. Put your dirty laundry in the hamper, not on the floor.

In addition to your room, perhaps you will be expected to help keep the rest of the house picked up. Does your mom or dad expect you to vacuum some of the rooms, and when? Are you ever to mop the kitchen floor, or just sweep it? Are you to wash dishes and put them away, or let them soak in soapy water in the sink? What are you to do about helping with the laundry, if anything, and when? In other words, make sure you know what you are to do and when you are to do it. If you are to operate any household appliances, such as a dishwasher, washing machine, clothes dryer, vacuum cleaner, etc., learn how they work and read Chapter 4.

Make a list of your weekly duties. After you have completed each task, cross it off your list. (This is a really satisfying thing to do!)

Put your radio or phonograph on and listen to music while you do household chores. Your work may go faster and more pleasantly.

KEEP THE HOUSE NEAT. Close all closet doors, dresser drawers and kitchen cabinets. Put dirty laundry in the hamper. Hang up your jacket or coat and put away your school books when you come home from school. If you change clothes after school, put away your school clothes in your dresser or closet. If you take a bath or shower, don't leave the bathroom looking as if a tidal wave had hit it. Hang up your towel, rinse the bathtub and sink. Put shampoo bottles, brushes, soap, etc. where they belong. If you wash small items in the bathroom sink, immediately hang them up to dry. Don't leave them soaking; other members of the family may need to use the sink.

If old newspapers and magazines have accumulated, stack them up in one neat pile, or throw them out if you have been told that the family no longer wants to read them. Old magazines can also be stored in a shopping bag or carton and later given to your local hospital, nursing home or day-care center. (If you like to make collages—pictures made of scraps of colorful magazine pages—you may want to save some old magazines for yourself. Keep them in a bag or on a shelf in your closet, or anywhere else where they will be out of sight.)

Sweep the kitchen and other floors whenever they look especially messy. This takes only a minute or two of your time and helps the house look neater. Wipe up spills or smudges you may have made on floors or walls right away, using a sponge with a little soap and water on it.

Do not wash a wooden floor, but if you have to wash a tile or a linoleum floor, fill a bucket half full with warm water. Add about a quarter cup of a liquid cleaner. Put the mop into the soap and water in the bucket. Make sure the mop is completely soaked through. Lift the mop and wring out excess water into the bucket. Wash a small area of the floor. Put the mop back into the bucket and swish it around. Wring out excess water again. Wash another small area of the floor. Repeat this procedure until the whole floor is done. Pour the dirty pail water into the toilet and flush it. Rinse the mop in clear water and wring it out. Put the bucket and mop away in the usual place.

LEARN ABOUT CLEANING SUPPLIES. If you are expected to use them, ask your mom or dad to explain to you which polish, spray, scouring powder or soap is meant for which job. Which is the furniture polish, and what liquid soap is to be used for mopping a floor or wiping dirty fingerprints from appliances or walls? If you know which is which, you will not use a window-cleaning spray on your living-room furniture, or the furniture polish for wiping off a grease stain on the kitchen counter. If you are still in doubt about any of these sprays, bottles and cans, make your own descriptive labels for each one of them.

Although each family likes to choose its own brands and variety of supplies, it is always good to have the following on hand: sal soda (washing soda); baking soda; furniture polish; window and mirror spray cleaner; cleaning liquid or powder for linoleum and other kitchen surfaces; washing-machine soap powder; dishwashing liquid and/or dishwasher soap powder; white vinegar (for washing out pet accident spots, see page 92); cornmeal.

WHAT TO DO IF SOMETHING SPILLS OR BREAKS. If you ever take food into the living room or one of the bedrooms and some of it spills, or if you break something, clean up right away. If a stain remains for a while on a rug or on a piece of upholstered furniture, it will be much harder to clean it later.

1. If you spill milk, ice cream or a soft drink on a rug or upholstered furniture, soak it up right away with paper towels or a clean rag. Then mix one cup of lukewarm water with about two tablespoons of sal soda. Moisten a clean, soft rag or sponge with it. Wring out the rag or sponge and rub the spot gently. Moisten the rag or sponge again in the soap and water, wring it out and rub again. You may need to do this a few times

until the spot disappears. Let the spot dry before you sit or walk on it.

2. If a chewed-up piece of chewing gum sticks to your rug or to an upholstered piece of furniture, here is what you do. Take an ice cube from your freezer and put it into a piece of paper towel or a rag. Rub the gum with it. The ice will harden the gum so that it can easily be peeled off.

3. If you get a grease stain on your rug or upholstered furniture, sprinkle some cornmeal on the stain and leave it there for a few hours. Afterward, vacuum up the cornmeal and the spot should disappear.

4. If you break a precious vase, bowl or knickknack, gather all the broken pieces and put them in a shoe box or other carton. Sometimes your parents, or a professional repairer, can glue the broken bits and pieces together and restore the item. If there are many sharp edges in the broken pieces, put on a pair of gloves or mittens before you pick them up. This will prevent your hands from being cut. Tell your parents when they come home about the accident. Give them the pieces of the broken object. Even some of the most precious broken things can be fixed or replaced, so don't despair over an accident. Next time, though, you might be more careful when you play in rooms where these objects are on display.

If you break an everyday glass or dish or cup, throw all the pieces into the trash right away. Sweep up the tiny bits and pieces which you cannot pick up by hand and throw them out as well.

IF YOU TAKE THE MAIL FROM YOUR MAIL-BOX before your parents return from work, don't hide it under a pile of school books or in your coat pocket or some other place where it is hard to find later. Decide on one place where the family mail should be kept and always put it there. A box hung on your kitchen or entrance hall wall is a good place to put the daily family mail. See page 12 for directions on making and decorating such a box.

IF YOU TAKE CLOTHES TO THE CLEANERS, look for loose change or other important things in the pockets. Even though one of your parents has undoubtedly done it too, there is no harm in double-checking. When you get the receipt from the cleaning shop, be sure that you put it in a prearranged place. In fact, it is a good idea to have one place in your house to keep receipts from cleaners, shoemakers or whatever. A specially made folder-file (see page 12) is really helpful. When you have one, receipts don't get lost and you don't have to search for them when the time comes to pick up your things. If you feel especially efficient, you may even want to put down on your family calendar the date on which the things should be picked up from the cleaners or the shoe-repair shop or wherever you are having something fixed.

TAKING CARE OF PLANTS, if your family has some, is one of the most pleasant chores there is. Find out how often the plants should be watered. Overwatering is as bad as not giving your plants enough water. Mist your plants with a special bottle made for this purpose. In city apartments, where the air is very dry, it is a good idea to mist the plants each day. Some people think that talking to plants is spooky, but there are others who believe that it helps. Anyway, talk to your plants while you water or mist them. They will not answer you, or scold you, or tell you what to do—but they may grow better because you have paid this special attention to them. If your plants can be clipped for cuttings and then planted in small pots, or rooted in cups of water, ask your parents whether you can sometimes do this.

There are many fine indoor-gardening books for young people. Borrow some of them from your library and learn more about tending household plants. A list of some titles can be found at the end of this book.

HELPING WITH MAJOR HOUSEHOLD CHORES each week when your parents are at home may be part of your duties. Cleaning out the refrigerator, vacuuming and dusting the whole house, straightening up closets and cabinets, dusting books or other major chores will go much faster when several people do them together. Discuss with your parents and your brothers and sisters how to divide these chores, or rotate them each week, so that each and every one of you has a fair share of the work.

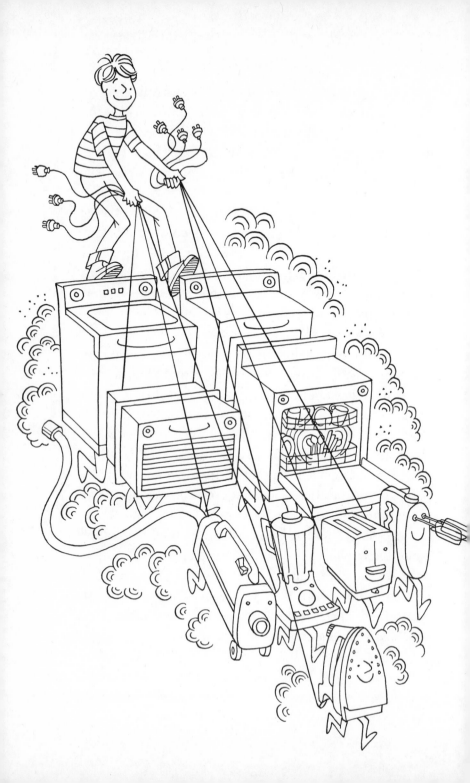

4 · Using Household Appliances

Ask your mom or dad to explain to you how household appliances—such as a washing machine, clothes dryer, dishwasher, toaster, blender, electric broiler, vacuum cleaner, mixer or iron—work. Do not try to use any of them unless you know what the different buttons on each of the appliances are meant to do. These appliances are costly to fix and expensive to buy, so do be careful when you use them.

If you notice that the appliances have frayed or torn cords, or broken or cracked plugs, don't use them. Tell your parent. A frayed or torn cord or a broken plug can cause a fire. Always disconnect any appliance after using it, unless it is permanently attached to the electrical socket with a grounding wire. When you disconnect an appliance, pull out the cord from the electrical socket by holding the plug, not the wire. Do not use long extension cords when you use an appliance. Plug in one appliance at a time in each of your electrical outlets. Overloading an electrical outlet can cause a short circuit, which may be hard for you to handle while your parents are away. Never plug in, or unplug, an appliance with wet hands. This can give you a bad shock.

If your family uses a coin-operated washing machine and dryer in a pay laundromat in your neighborhood or in the basement laundry room in the building where you live, and you have permission to use them, ask your mom or dad to show you how they work too.

Here are some tips on using various household appliances. These suggestions however are *in addition* to what you have learned from one of your parents. If one of your appliances doesn't work, tell your mom or dad.

VACUUM CLEANER. If you know how to plug in your vacuum cleaner, how to change the vacuum-cleaner bags if they are full and what attachments and brushes are meant for which jobs, here are a few additional tips:

1. Be sure the bag that collects the dust in your vacuum cleaner is not completely full. If it is full, take it out and put in a new one.

2. If you vacuum a rug, be sure that you have the correct attachment on the machine. If you are vacuuming a floor, attach the proper brush for that.

3. Vacuum a small area at a time. Do not try to vacuum an area that is larger than about four square feet. Do a small part of the room at a time. When you are finished with that part, go on to the next. There is no harm if there is some overlapping in the areas you are cleaning.

4. Do not vacuum desk tops, bookcases, knickknack shelves or any other surfaces on which you have small objects. The machine will pull them all in. In fact, it will "eat up" socks, pencils, small toys, etc. Take small objects off the floor too before you clean.

5. If you have broken something, do not vacuum up chunks of broken glass, china or whatever. These sharp bits and pieces of broken objects can ruin the vacuum hose and break the motor as well.

6. Never vacuum a wet floor. The suction will pull in water and as a result the motor and the vacuum hose will need to be replaced.

WASHING MACHINE. If you are supposed to wash laundry either in your own washing machine or in a coin-operated one, and you know how to use the machine, here are a few additional tips:

1. Never put white and colored clothing to wash together. Colored clothing, such as dark socks, jeans, sport shirts, etc., may let out color and ruin your white clothes. Wash them separately.

2. Do not put too many clothes in the machine at the same time. They won't come out clean if the machine is overloaded. Overloading is also bad for the machine motor.

3. Do not put in too much soap powder. Too many suds do not make a cleaner load of laundry, and they are hard to rinse out. Do not put more than ¾ cup of soap powder into a washing machine.

4. Do not put in laundry bleach with colored clothing. It is hard for you to know which of the things are colorfast and which aren't. Laundry bleach may remove the color from your clothing.

5. If your mom or dad uses it, add fabric softener when the machine is on the rinse cycle.

6. If you wash in a coin-operated machine, put socks

in a mesh bag from the dime store. Washing them in a mesh bag keeps them together so you will not lose any. You can dry the socks right in the mesh bag too.

CLOTHES DRYER. If you know how to operate your dryer or the dryer in the coin-operated laundry or in the laundry room of the building where you live, here are a few hints:

1. Do not put a lot of wet clothing at one time into the dryer. Load the dryer only about half full. This will give room for the wet laundry to tumble. If you stuff too much laundry into the dryer, it will come out very wrinkled. It is better to divide the laundry into two loads for drying than to have it come out wrinkled, and possibly damp as well.

2. When the laundry is dry, take it out of the dryer right away and fold it into your laundry basket or laundry bag. If you have a dryer in your own home, and your mom or dad says it is all right for you to leave clothes in the dryer until one of them returns home, do that. However, folding laundry can be a really peaceful, pleasant kind of job—especially if you listen to music at the same time.

DISHWASHER. If you know how to operate your dishwasher and how your mom or dad wants you to handle it, go ahead and use it. Here are a few hints:

1. Scrape or rinse all the food from the plates before you put them into the dishwasher.

2. Always put the big plates at the bottom of the

dishwasher. Smaller plates, cups, saucers and glasses can go on the top rack of the dishwasher.

3. If you have pots and pans along with dishes to put into the dishwasher, rinse them well under running water. Put them next to the large plates on the bottom of the dishwasher.

4. Do not put plastic or wooden bowls, spoons, cups, etc. into a dishwasher. The heat of the machine will crack the wood and melt the plastic items. Melted plastic can also ruin the dishwasher itself.

5. Only use soap powder that is meant for the dishwasher. You will have a big mess if you put laundry detergent into the dishwasher instead of the dishwashing powder. There may be so many suds that they will ooze out of the machine. However, if such a calamity happens, here is what you do. Turn the dishwasher off. Open it. Put in one full cup of fabric softener such as Downy, Nu-Soft or whatever your family uses. Turn on the dishwasher again. The fabric softener should make the laundry-detergent suds disappear. If this does not work completely the first time around, repeat the whole procedure again. The suds will surely disappear on your second try, and the dishes will not be hurt by the laundry softener.

BLENDER. After you have learned from your mom or dad just how your blender works, here are a few things to remember:

1. If your blender came with a booklet of recipes and instructions, read them. Many of the recipes in the

booklets that come with blenders are very good and easy to prepare.

2. Do not put too much into the blender at one time.

3. Do not let the blender run for a long time. A minute or two is all that's needed.

4. If your blender has a glass container, do not put in anything very, very hot. It may crack the glass.

5. If you have to mix anything in the blender with a spoon or rubber spatula, turn off the motor. Never try to stir anything in a blender while it is on. You can break the blender blades and/or your mixing utensil.

6. Disconnect the blender from the electrical outlet before you take off the container to pour out whatever you have made in it.

MIXER. Since I happen to think baking is the most fun and most interesting thing to do in the kitchen, I'd urge you to learn how to use your family's mixer if you have one. There are two types of mixers—the portable kind and the standing kind. They both do the same work, but the portable mixer must be held in your hand while you use it, and the standing one can be left to mix all by itself. If you know how to use your family's mixer, here are a few additional hints:

1. Put the moving attachments into the mixer before you plug it into your electrical outlet. It is safer to attach parts of an electrical appliance before it is plugged in.

2. Turn off the mixer motor before you lift the attachments out of whatever you are mixing. If you do not

turn off the mixer, you will have batter, or whatever, all over the walls, ceiling, floor and counter.

3. Stop the mixer before you stir the batter or whatever you are adding to it. The blades of the mixer can be ruined if they hit your mixing spoon. Your fingers can also get hurt. Scrape the batter off the sides of your mixing bowl with a wooden spoon or plastic spatula. Then turn the mixer on again and continue until all is done.

IRON. It is a good idea to know how to use an iron, so ask your mom or dad how it works. Then if you need to press something in a hurry while your mom or dad is gone, you will know just what to do. Here are a few additional tips:

1. Use an ironing board for ironing if you have one.

If you do not have an ironing board, put several towels or a blanket on top of your kitchen table, washing machine or counter. Press your clothing or whatever on top of the towels or blanket.

2. Plug in the iron and stand it on end. Set the control to the required temperature. (If you are ironing all by yourself, it might be safer to set the control for the temperature marked "wool.") Let the iron preheat for about three minutes.

3. Move the iron with quick, even strokes back and forth over the fabric you are ironing. Do not let the iron stand on the material you are ironing, for it may scorch the fabric.

4. As soon as you have finished ironing, disconnect the iron from the electrical outlet. Do not put it back in its box or closet or wherever it is kept until it is completely cool.

TOASTER. The toaster is one machine which you surely know how to use without a bit of help. However, remember the following:

1. If you have a regular toaster—not a toaster oven— do not make anything in it but dry toast. Don't butter the bread before you put it in, don't make grilled-cheese sandwiches in it, don't try anything fancy. An ordinary toaster is meant to make ordinary toast—and a good thing it is.

2. If you have a toaster oven, ask your parents to tell you what it can do. The advantages of a toaster oven are that you can make grilled-cheese sandwiches,

muffin pizzas and even heat up a small pan of food in it. Learn how to use it to best advantage.

AIR CONDITIONER. If you have your parent's permission to use the air conditioner in your home, and you know just how it works, it is still a good idea to remember the following:

1. Make sure that all the windows in the room are closed. You want to cool your rooms, not the streets!

2. Turn the air conditioner on to "Fan" first. Let it run on "Fan" for at least three minutes.

3. After it has been on "Fan" for a few minutes, switch to "Cool."

4. If you leave the room and do not expect to return soon, turn the air conditioner off. If, for some reason, you must immediately turn it on again, be sure to give it *five minutes' rest* before you turn on the motor. Start again with "Fan" for a few minutes, then switch to "Cool."

5 · Preparing Meals

Planning menus for the week and shopping for food with your family can be as much fun as reading a detective story. When the supermarkets feature certain foods on sale, look up recipes in cookbooks and see how they can be prepared. Your family may have some cookbooks in the house, or you can borrow some from the library. There are also many wonderful cookbooks written especially for young cooks (see the list at the end of this book). Read them to become familiar with the "mysteries" of cooking—though cooking isn't mysterious at all. There are many, many ways to prepare all kinds of foods, and the more you learn about these ways, the more interesting and enjoyable meals will be.

Above all else, you will find that planning and cooking meals is really creative and very satisfying work. Learning to prepare meals and to shop for food when you are young will be helpful to you for the rest of your life. Ask your mother or your father to teach you what she or he knows, to take you marketing and to let you help plan the family's menus.

Starting meals before one of your parents comes home from work can save him or her a great deal of time. This "found" time can be spent doing things together when your mom or dad is home.

Perhaps you are not expected to do anything more

than to put a previously prepared casserole into a 350° oven at a specific hour in the afternoon. If that is all you have to do to start a meal, then be sure to remember the hour when you are supposed to do it. Put a reminder note on your calendar or work schedule for that day, or attach it to the refrigerator. Maybe all you need to do is to wash and drain the salad greens a half-hour before your parents are expected home. Or maybe just set the table. Every little bit helps.

When there is no previously prepared meal to be put into the oven or on the stove and you have kindly offered to cook a meal all by yourself from beginning to end, or together with a brother or sister, you may want to try some interesting recipes from various cookbooks, or the recipes in this chapter. Those given here are, by and large, easy to prepare in a reasonably short time, and many of them do not even need to be cooked. Some of the main-course recipes for dinner do require cooking, but these are simple and easy to fix. Suggestions are also given for some after-school snacks and box lunches.

Read a recipe on the day before you plan to prepare it. Check to see whether you have at home everything you will need. If you do not have some of the necessary ingredients, substitute a dish for which you do have everything at home, or ask your mom or dad whether you may buy the missing ingredients. Make sure that the weights or sizes of cans required in a recipe are the ones you have on hand.

Wash your hands and put on an apron before you

start cooking. Be exact in following each recipe and be careful when you use knives, can openers, beaters or whatever. Set out all the equipment you will need. Line up all the ingredients on your working surface.

If you make a mess while you are working, clean it up right away. Wipe off sticky fingerprints from the refrigerator, counter tops and stove. Wipe up spills from the floor and counter tops before they get sticky and messy. Don't let dirty utensils and bowls pile up on your table or counter. Put them into the dishwasher, if you have one, or in soapy water in the sink.

If grease catches fire in a frying pan, pour baking soda on it. Don't pour water over burning grease—it will splatter and hiss and make a mess.

Here is a list of menus for five dinners and two weekend lunches, followed by recipes for the dishes marked with asterisks. The recipes are divided into three groups—Appetizers and Soups, Main Courses and Desserts. If you don't like one of the dishes in a menu, you can substitute another you like better from the same group of recipes or from a cookbook.

DINNER MENUS

Monday
Grapefruit Cups with Honey*
Sweet and Sour Chicken with Rice*
Green salad
Chocolate Mint Pudding*

Tuesday
Tomato-Sour Cream Soup*
Egg, Corn and Cheese Puff*
Chocolate Cookies in Cream*

Wednesday
Fruit Cocktail*
Fish Fillets and Potatoes in Cream Sauce*
Sliced tomatoes
Cranberry Whip*

Thursday
Gazpacho (Spanish Soup)*
Ham and Pineapple Salad*
Rolls or bread and butter
Applesauce with Sour Cream*

Friday
Chilled Cream of Chicken Soup*
Meatball and Rice Casserole*
Green salad
Banana-Prune Whip*

LUNCH MENUS FOR WEEKENDS

Saturday
Salmon Salad*
Rolls and butter
Clowns for Dessert*

Sunday
Fried Ham and Cheese Sandwiches*
Sliced tomatoes
Apple Cake Dessert*

APPETIZERS AND SOUPS

Grapefruit Cups with Honey (for 4 people)

You will need: *Use:*
2 seedless grapefruits   Cutting knife
4 tablespoons of honey   Curved grapefruit-
                                         sectioning knife
                                         Measuring spoon or
                                         tablespoon

Prepare it this way:
1. Cut each of the 2 grapefruits in half.
2. Using a curved grapefruit-sectioning knife, cut around the grapefruit halves, near the rinds. Make sure that the knife cuts deeply around the center

of the grapefruit, as well as near the rind, so that you will be able to get all the fruit out of the rind when you eat it.

3. Cut along each side of the grapefruit sections to separate them from the pulp. Leave the sections in the grapefruit rind shells.

4. Pour 1 tablespoon of honey over each of the grapefruit halves. Just before serving the grapefruit, put the halves into a 300°F. oven for about 5 minutes.

Fruit Cocktail (for 4 people)

You will need:	Use:
1 medium (16-ounce) can of fruit cocktail	Can opener
	Large bowl
1 banana	Knife
1 apple	Paper towels
4 tablespoons of raisins	Measuring spoon
4 tablespoons of ginger ale	Mixing spoon
	Aluminum foil
	4 cereal or fruit bowls

Prepare it this way:

1. Open the can of fruit cocktail. Pour all the fruit cocktail with the syrup into the large bowl.

2. Peel 1 banana and slice it. Add the banana slices to the bowl with the fruit cocktail.

3. Wash the apple. Dry it with paper towels. Cut the apple in half. Cut the halves in half again. You will have 4 quarters. Cut out the cores from the apple quarters. Throw away the cores. Cut the apple

quarters in small pieces. Add the apple pieces to
the fruit cocktail.

4. Add 4 tablespoons of raisins to the fruit cocktail.
Mix all fruits in the bowl with a mixing spoon.
Cover the bowl with aluminum foil. Put the bowl
of fruit cocktail in the refrigerator for about 2
hours.

5. Add 4 tablespoons of ginger ale to the fruit cocktail just before you serve it. Mix the fruit cocktail
with the soda. Put the fruit cocktail in 4 cereal or
fruit bowls. Serve.

Gazpacho (Spanish Soup) (for 4–6 people)

You will need:
1 10½-ounce can of con-
densed tomato soup
1 10½-ounce can of con-
densed consommé
1½ cans of cold water
1 cucumber
1 green pepper
1 tomato
1 onion
2 tablespoons of fresh
or bottled lemon juice
¼ teaspoon of pepper
¼ teaspoon of garlic
powder
Dash of Tabasco sauce

Use:
Can opener
Large bowl
Mixing spoon
Paper towels
Knife
Measuring spoons
Aluminum foil
Soup bowls

Prepare it this way:

1. Open the 2 cans of soup. Pour the soups into a large bowl. Add 1½ cans of cold water. Mix the 2 soups and the water with a mixing spoon until well blended.

2. Wash the cucumber, pepper and tomato. Dry them with paper towels. Cut the cucumber into thin slices. Add the cucumber slices to the bowl with the soup.

3. Cut the green pepper in half. Scoop out the seeds and the pulp. Use your hands to do this. Throw away the seeds and the pulp. Cut the pepper halves into small pieces. Add them to the soup.

4. Cut the tomato into small pieces. Add them to the soup.

5. Cut the onion in half. Save one half of the onion (wrap it in waxed paper or foil and put it in the refrigerator). Peel the other half of the onion. Cut it into small pieces. Add them to the soup in the bowl.

6. Now add to the soup 2 tablespoons of lemon juice, ¼ teaspoon of pepper, ¼ teaspoon of garlic powder and a dash of Tabasco. Mix all the things in the bowl very well with a mixing spoon. Cover the bowl with aluminum foil. Put it into the refrigerator for at least 2 hours. Pour into soup bowls. Serve.

Tomato-Sour Cream Soup *(for 4 people)*

You will need:	*Use:*
2 10½-ounce cans of tomato soup	Can opener Large bowl

1 cup of sour cream   Measuring cup
1 cup of cold water   Mixing spoon
½ cucumber   Large plate or
16 salty crackers   aluminum foil
                             Knife
                             4 soup bowls

Prepare it this way:
1. Open both cans of soup and pour the soup into the bowl. Measure 1 cup of sour cream and add it to the soup. Stir slowly until the sour cream is well mixed with the soup.
2. Add 1 cup of cold water slowly to the soup and sour cream, stirring until it is all mixed together. Cover the bowl with a plate or aluminum foil and put into the refrigerator for at least 1 hour.
3. Just before serving, peel ½ cucumber. Cut the cucumber into thin slices and add to the soup. Pour the soup into the soup bowls and serve with salty crackers.

Chilled Cream of Chicken Soup *(for 4 people)*

You will need: *Use:*
1 10½-ounce can of   Can opener
   cream of chicken   Large bowl
   soup   Sieve
1 8-ounce jar or can   Mixing spoon
   of applesauce   Measuring cup
1½ cups of milk   Rotary beater or electric
¼ teaspoon of salt   mixer

¼ teaspoon of white
   pepper
¼ teaspoon of curry
   powder

Measuring spoon
Large plate or aluminum
   foil
4 soup bowls

Prepare it this way:

1. Open the can of cream of chicken soup. Put the sieve over the bowl and pour the soup into the sieve.
2. Open the jar or can of applesauce and add it to the soup in the sieve.
3. With the mixing spoon, stir the soup and apple-sauce mixture in the sieve until it all goes through into the bowl. You will have a few pieces of chicken left in the sieve; throw them out or give them to your dog or cat.
4. Very slowly, add a little of the 1½ cups of milk to the soup and applesauce mixture. Mix it in with the rotary beater or electric mixer. Then add a little more milk and beat again. Do this until you have added all the milk and the soup looks nice and smooth.
5. Add ¼ teaspoon of salt, ¼ teaspoon of white pepper and ¼ teaspoon of curry powder and mix well with the spoon.
6. Cover the bowl with a plate or aluminum foil and put it into the refrigerator for at least 2 hours. When the soup is very cold, pour it into the soup bowls and serve. Pass around salt and pepper, in case your family or friends like their soup to be more spicy.

MAIN COURSES

Ham and Pineapple Salad (for 4 people)

You will need:

1 16-ounce can of pine-
  apple chunks
1 cup of chopped
  celery (about 3 large
  stalks)
1 4-ounce package of
  sliced ham
½ cup of mayonnaise
¼ teaspoon of creamy
  mustard
1 teaspoon of honey
½ teaspoon of fresh or
  bottled lemon juice
4 lettuce leaves
4 hard rolls and butter

Use:

Can opener
Small bowl
Sieve
Bowl for salad
Paper towels
Knife
Measuring cup
Mixing spoon
Measuring spoons
Aluminum foil
4 dinner plates

Prepare it this way:

1. Open the can of pineapple chunks. Put the sieve
   over a small bowl. Put the pineapple chunks into
   the sieve. Let the syrup drain off the pineapple.
   Shake the sieve a few times to help the syrup drain
   off. Put the pineapple chunks into the salad bowl.
   Save the syrup for making a gelatin dessert.
2. Wash 3 large stalks of celery. Cut off the leaves
   from the celery stalks. Dry the celery stalks with
   paper towels. Cut the celery stalks into small pieces.
   Put them in a measuring cup. When the cup is full,

put the celery pieces in the bowl with the pine-apple chunks.

3. Open the package of sliced ham. Cut the ham slices into thin strips. Put the ham strips into the bowl with the pineapple chunks and celery pieces. Mix with a mixing spoon.

4. Measure ½ cup of mayonnaise. Add to the mayonnaise ¼ teaspoon of creamy mustard, 1 teaspoon of honey and ½ teaspoon of lemon juice. Mix the mayonnaise with the mustard, honey and lemon juice. Use a mixing spoon.

5. Put the mayonnaise into the bowl with the ham, pineapple chunks and celery. Mix them all well with the mixing spoon. Cover the bowl with aluminum foil. Put the bowl of salad in the refrigerator for 1 hour.

6. Just before you serve the salad, wash 4 lettuce leaves under cold running water in the sink. Shake off the water from the lettuce leaves. Pat them dry with a paper towel. Put 1 lettuce leaf on each plate. Put salad on top of each of the lettuce leaves. Serve with hard rolls and butter.

Salmon Salad (for 4 people)

You will need:	Use:
1 can (7¾ ounces) of salmon	Can opener Sieve
1 cup of chopped celery (about 3 large stalks)	Bowl Paper towels
1 cucumber	Knife

½ cup of mayonnaise
1 tablespoon of fresh
  or bottled lemon juice
¼ teaspoon of salt
4 lettuce leaves
Seeded rolls and butter

Measuring cup
Measuring spoons
Mixing spoon
Aluminum foil
4 dinner plates

Prepare it this way:

1. Open the can of salmon. Hold the sieve over the sink. Put the salmon into the sieve. Let the oil drain off the salmon. Shake the sieve a few times to help the oil drain off. Put the salmon into the bowl.

2. Wash 3 large stalks of celery. Cut off the leaves from the celery stalks. Dry the celery stalks with paper towels. Cut the celery stalks into small pieces. Put them in a measuring cup. When the cup is full, put the celery pieces in the bowl with the salmon.

3. Peel the cucumber. Cut it into small pieces. Add the pieces of cucumber to the bowl with the salmon and celery.

4. Add ½ cup of mayonnaise to the bowl with the salmon. Add 1 tablespoon of lemon juice to the bowl. Add ¼ teaspoon of salt to the bowl. Mix the salmon, celery and cucumber with the mayonnaise. Use a mixing spoon. Cover the bowl with aluminum foil. Put the bowl of salad into the refrigerator for 1 hour.

5. Just before you serve the salad, wash 4 lettuce leaves under cold running water in the sink. Pat them dry with a paper towel. Put 1 lettuce leaf on

each plate. Put salmon salad on top of each of the
lettuce leaves. Serve with seeded rolls and butter.

Egg, Corn and Cheese Puff (for 4 people)

You will need:	Use:
6 eggs	Large bowl
¾ cup of milk	Whisk or fork
1 teaspoon of salt	Measuring cup
⅛ teaspoon of pepper	Measuring spoons
¼ teaspoon of dried basil	Can opener
1 teaspoon of dried chopped parsley	Sieve
	Small bowl
1 cup of canned whole-kernel corn, drained (from 1-pound 1-ounce can)	Spoon
	Knife
	Paper towel or napkin
	Baking dish or casserole
1 cup of cubed cheese, such as Swiss, cheddar, muenster or a combination of all of them	
½ cup of diced sandwich meat, such as ham, salami or bologna (optional)	
1 teaspoon of butter	

Prepare it this way:
1. Preheat oven to 350° F.
2. Crack the eggs and put them into a large bowl. Add
   ¾ cup of milk to the eggs in the bowl. Beat the eggs
   and milk with a whisk or fork to mix them well.

3. Add 1 teaspoon of salt, ⅛ teaspoon of pepper, ¼ teaspoon of dried basil and 1 teaspoon of dried chopped parsley to the milk and egg mixture. Beat again with whisk or fork.

4. Open the can of corn. A 1-pound 1-ounce can has more than you will need. Put the sieve over a small bowl. Pour the contents of the can of corn into the sieve. Using a spoon, take out enough drained corn from the sieve to fill one cup. Add the cup of corn to the egg and milk mixture in the large bowl. Mix with fork or whisk.

5. Put the remaining corn in the sieve into the small bowl with the corn juice. Cover and refrigerate for use later on.

6. Cut up enough Swiss, cheddar or muenster cheese chunks, or a combination of all three, to fill one cup. Add the cheese to the mixture in the large bowl. Mix with fork or whisk.

7. If you have ham, salami or bologna in the house, cut enough into small pieces to fill ½ cup. Add this cut-up sandwich meat to the bowl. Mix with fork or whisk. (The puff will taste good even without the meat, but do add it if you have it.)

8. Butter a baking dish or casserole. If you have never buttered a baking dish, here is what you do. Put one teaspoon of butter on a piece of clean paper towel or on a paper napkin. Rub the butter all over the bottom and sides of the baking dish or casserole. This will prevent the mixture from sticking to the dish.

9. Pour the egg, milk, corn, cheese, etc. mixture into

the buttered baking dish or casserole. Bake for about 40 minutes in the oven, or until the top is puffy and golden brown.

Fried Ham and Cheese Sandwiches (for 4 people)

You will need:

Use:

8 slices of white bread

8 slices of ham (or other sandwich meat such as bologna, salami, etc.)

4 slices of American or Swiss cheese

2 eggs

3 tablespoons of milk

4 tablespoons of margarine or butter

Mixing bowl

Measuring spoons

Fork

Large frying pan

Spatula

Prepare it this way:

1. Put 4 slices of white bread on your working surface. Put 2 slices of ham and 1 slice of cheese on each of the 4 slices of bread. Put the remaining 4 slices of bread over each of the ham-and-cheese-covered pieces of bread.
2. Crack the 2 eggs and put them into a bowl. Add 3 tablespoons of milk to the eggs in the bowl. Beat with fork to mix the milk and eggs together.
3. Put a large frying pan over medium heat on your stove. Add 4 tablespoons of margarine or butter to the frying pan.

4. When the margarine or butter is sizzly, dip each of the sandwiches you have made into the milk and egg mixture. Make sure that both sides have been dipped into the egg and milk mixture. Put them in the frying pan. If the pan is too small for four sandwiches, fry two at a time.

5. Cook over a medium flame for about 5 minutes. Using a spatula, turn each sandwich over on the other side and cook for about 3 minutes longer. By this time the cheese inside the sandwich will be melted and the whole sandwich will be quite delicious—sort of a combination of French toast and a grilled cheese and ham sandwich. Very filling and good, not only for lunch but for supper as well. Delicious with sliced tomatoes.

Fish Fillets and Potatoes in Cream Sauce (for 4 people)

You will need:

Use:

1 to 1½ pounds of fish fillets (flounder, sole or scrod)

4 medium potatoes

1 10½-ounce can of cream of vegetable or cream of celery soup

¼ cup of milk

½ teaspoon of salt

¼ teaspoon of pepper

½ teaspoon of paprika

Paper towels
Toothpicks
Flat baking dish
   or casserole
Knife
Can opener
Mixing bowls
Measuring cup
Measuring spoons
Spoon

Prepare it this way:

1. Preheat oven to 350° F.
2. Wash the fish fillets under cold running water. Pat them dry with paper towels. Make sure that no pieces of paper towel stick to the fish fillets.
3. Roll up the fish fillets. Stick a toothpick into each rolled fillet. Put the fillets into a flat baking dish or casserole.
4. Peel 4 medium potatoes. Cut the potatoes into very small pieces. Arrange the potatoes around the fish fillets in the baking dish.
5. Open the can of creamed vegetable or celery soup. Pour the contents of the can into a small mixing bowl. Add ¼ cup of milk, ½ teaspoon of salt and ¼ teaspoon of pepper to the soup in the bowl. Mix it all very well with a mixing spoon. Pour this mixture over the fish fillets and potatoes in the baking dish.
6. Sprinkle about ½ teaspoon of paprika over the whole thing.
7. Put the casserole into preheated oven. Bake the fish and potatoes for about 35 minutes.

Sweet and Sour Chicken with Rice *(for 4 people)*

You will need:	Use:
1 frying chicken, cut up in pieces	Paper towels
	Flat baking dish or casserole
1 small (11-ounce) can of mandarin oranges	Can opener
½ jar (10 ounces) of sweet and sour sauce	Bowl
	Measuring spoons

1 tablespoon of soy
sauce
½ teaspoon of salt
¼ teaspoon of pepper
1⅓ cups of instant rice

Mixing spoon
Measuring cup
Oven mitts or
pot holders

Prepare it this way:
1. Preheat oven to 350° F.
2. Wash chicken pieces under cold running water. Pat them dry with paper towels. Make sure that no pieces of paper towel stick to the chicken.
3. Put the chicken in a baking dish or casserole.
4. Open the can of mandarin oranges. Pour the contents of the can into a bowl. Add ½ jar of sweet and sour sauce, 1 tablespoon of soy sauce, ½ teaspoon of salt and ¼ teaspoon of pepper to the mandarin oranges in the bowl. Mix it all very well.
5. Pour this mixture over the chicken pieces in the baking dish or casserole. Put the casserole in oven.
6. After about 30 minutes, open the oven. Using pot holders or oven mitts, take out the casserole. Baste the chicken pieces with the sauce. Put the casserole back into the oven for another 30 minutes.
7. About 10 minutes before you are ready to eat, prepare 1⅓ cup of instant rice according to directions on the package.

Meatball and Rice Casserole (for 4 people)

You will need:
1 pound of hamburger
meat

Use:
Mixing bowl
Measuring cup

2 small envelopes of
   Cup-a-Soup instant
   onion soup mix
½ cup of dry bread crumbs
½ cup of milk
1 egg
¼ teaspoon of pepper
2 tablespoons of oil
¼ cup of flour
1 10½-ounce can of beef
   consommé
¼ cup of water
1⅓ cups of instant rice

2 small bowls
Measuring spoons
Mixing spoon
Frying pan
Can opener
2-quart covered
   casserole

Prepare it this way:

1. Preheat oven to 350° F.
2. Put the hamburger meat into the mixing bowl. Add the contents of two envelopes of Cup-a-Soup onion soup mix to the meat. (There is a difference between the sizes of the regular onion soup mix envelopes and the Cup-a-Soup packages, so be sure to use the right kind. Otherwise the meat will be too salty.)
3. Put ½ cup of bread crumbs into one of the small bowls. Add ½ cup of milk to the bread crumbs. Let the bread crumbs soak in the milk for a minute or two.
4. Crack and add 1 egg to the meat-and-onion-soup mixture. Add about ¼ teaspoon of pepper.
5. Add the soaked bread crumbs to the meat. Mix the meat mixture thoroughly with a large mixing

spoon. You can use your hands to mix the meat, if you wash them carefully before.

6. Put the frying pan over low heat on your stove. Pour 2 tablespoons of oil into the frying pan.
7. Put ¼ cup of flour in the other small bowl. Make small meatballs out of the meat mixture. Roll each meatball in a little flour.
8. Fry the meatballs a few at a time in the hot oil.
9. Open the can of consommé and pour it into the casserole. Add ¼ cup of water to the consommé. Measure out 1⅓ cups of instant rice and add it to the consommé in the casserole. Place meatballs on top of the rice. Cover the casserole.
10. Put the casserole into the oven for about 45 minutes. The rice will be soft and plump by then and the meatballs all cooked through.

DESSERTS

Chocolate Cookies in Cream (for 4 people)

You will need:
20 Hydrox or Oreo
     cookies
1 cup of heavy cream
2 tablespoons of
     confectioners' sugar
½ teaspoon of vanilla
     extract
4 cherries or
     strawberries

Use:
Dinner plate
Measuring cup
Mixing bowl
Measuring spoons
Rotary beater or
     electric mixer
Mixing spoon
4 dessert bowls

Prepare it this way:

1. Break the 20 Hydrox or Oreo cookies into small pieces. Put the cookie pieces on a dinner plate.
2. Put 1 cup of heavy cream into mixing bowl. Add 2 tablespoons of confectioners' sugar. Add ½ teaspoon of vanilla extract. To make whipped cream, beat the heavy cream with a rotary beater or an electric mixer for a few minutes. (If you use a rotary beater, it will take about 5 to 7 minutes to whip the cream; if you use an electric mixer, it will take about 2 to 3 minutes to whip the cream. If you whip heavy cream too long, it will become butter, so time this carefully.)
3. Put the cookie pieces into the bowl with the whipped cream. Mix the whipped cream with the cookie pieces. Use a mixing spoon.
4. Put the whipped cream with the cookie pieces in 4 dessert bowls. Put a fresh cherry or strawberry, or a maraschino cherry, on top of each dessert bowl. Serve.

Chocolate Mint Pudding *(for 4 people)*

You will need:
1 package of instant chocolate pudding
2 cups of milk
12 dessert chocolate mints

Use:
Mixing bowl
Measuring cup
Rotary beater or electric mixer
Mixing spoon
Aluminum foil
4 dessert bowls

Prepare it this way:

1. Put the instant chocolate pudding into mixing bowl. Slowly add 2 cups of cold milk to the pudding. Mix the pudding with a rotary beater or electric mixer as you add the milk. Keep on mixing the pudding for about 3 minutes after all the milk is in it.

2. Break 8 chocolate dessert mints into small pieces. Save the other 4 mints. Put the mint pieces into the pudding. With a spoon, mix the pudding together with the mint pieces. Cover the bowl with aluminum foil. Put in the refrigerator for about 2 hours.

3. Take the pudding out of the refrigerator. Divide it with a mixing spoon into 4 dessert bowls. Put a whole chocolate mint on top of each of the dessert bowls. Serve right away.

Cranberry Whip *(for 4 people)*

You will need:	*Use:*
2 eggs	2 teacups or small bowls
1 tablespoon of milk or water	Mixing bowl
	Measuring spoons
1 16-ounce can (2 cups) whole cranberry sauce	1 small plate or aluminum foil
	Rotary beater or electric mixer
4 tablespoons of chopped walnuts	Can opener
	Mixing spoon
	1 large plate or aluminum foil
	4 dessert bowls

Prepare it this way:

1. Separate the egg whites from the egg yolks this way: Crack 1 egg by tapping it gently against the edge of a teacup or small bowl. Hold the cracked egg over the cup or bowl and let the white drip into it. When all the white has dripped into the cup, put the egg yolk into another cup or bowl. Put the white into the mixing bowl. Crack the other egg over the cup and add the white to the first one. Put the second yolk into the cup or bowl with the first yolk. Put 1 tablespoon of milk (or water) over the egg yolks so they won't dry out. Cover the cup or bowl with a small plate or aluminum foil, and store in the refrigerator. You will not need the yolks in this recipe but you or your mother or father will be able to use them later.

2. Beat the 2 egg whites with the rotary beater or electric mixer until they are stiff and stand in peaks.

3. Open the can of whole cranberry sauce and fold the cranberry sauce into the egg whites this way: With the mixing spoon, place some of the cranberry sauce on top of the egg whites in the bowl and gently lift some of the egg white from the bottom of the bowl over the cranberry sauce. Repeat until the cranberry sauce is mixed into the egg whites. Then add some more cranberry sauce and fold it in the same way. Keep doing this until you have added all the cranberry sauce.

4. Add 4 tablespoons of chopped walnuts and mix them lightly with the cranberry-and-egg-white mixture.

5. Cover the mixing bowl with a large plate or aluminum foil and chill in the refrigerator for at least 2
hours. Then serve it in the dessert bowls.

Applesauce with Sour Cream *(for 4 people)*

You will need:

2 8-ounce jars or cans
   of applesauce
½ cup of sour cream
1 tablespoon of brown
   sugar
1 teaspoon of fresh or
   bottled lemon juice

Use:

Can opener
1 big mixing bowl
Measuring cup
Measuring spoon
Mixing spoon
4 dessert bowls

Prepare it this way:

1. Open the jars or cans of applesauce, and put the
applesauce into the big mixing bowl.
2. Measure ½ cup of sour cream, 1 tablespoon of
brown sugar and 1 teaspoon of lemon juice. Add
these to the bowl with the applesauce. Mix well
with the spoon and put into the refrigerator for at
least 1 hour. Then you are ready to serve in the
dessert bowls.

Apple Cake Dessert *(for 8 people)*

You will need:

1 angel cake or chiffon
   cake from the super-
   market
2¼ cups of milk

Use:

Mixing bowl
Measuring cup
Rotary beater or
   electric mixer

1 package of instant   Knife
   vanilla pudding   Pretty serving bowl
1 can (1 pound 5 ounces)   Can opener
   of apple pie filling   Aluminum foil
                              8 dessert plates

Prepare it this way:

1. Put the instant vanilla pudding powder into the mixing bowl. Slowly add 2¼ cups of cold milk to the powder. Mix with a rotary beater or electric mixer as you add the milk. Keep on mixing the pudding for about 3 minutes after all the milk is in it.
2. Cut the angel or chiffon cake in half. Cut one half of the cake into small pieces. They should be about ½ inch by ½ inch in size.
3. Put the cake pieces in the bottom of a pretty serving bowl.
4. Open the can of apple pie filling. Put the pie filling all over the cake pieces in the dessert bowl.
5. Now cut the other half of the chiffon or angel cake into small pieces. They should also be about ½ inch by ½ inch in size.
6. Put the cake pieces all over the pie filling in the dessert bowl.
7. Pour the vanilla pudding over the cake and apple pie filling in the dessert bowl. Cover the dessert bowl with aluminum foil. Put it in the refrigerator for several hours. Serve on dessert plates. Since this recipe serves 8 people, you will have enough in case friends or family drop in.

Banana-Prune Whip (for 4 people)

You will need:	Use:
½ cup of heavy cream	Measuring cup
2 tablespoons of confectioners' sugar	2 mixing bowls
	Measuring spoons
2 very ripe bananas	Rotary beater or electric
1 cup of strained baby food prunes	mixer
	Fork
1 teaspoon of fresh or bottled lemon juice	Mixing spoon
	1 large plate
	4 dessert bowls

Prepare it this way:

1. Put ½ cup of heavy cream into one of the mixing bowls. Add 2 tablespoons of confectioners' sugar to the cream, and beat it with the rotary beater or electric mixer for a few minutes. (See instructions on whipping cream in recipe for Chocolate Cookies in Cream.)
2. Peel the bananas and put them in the other bowl. Mash them with the fork. The bananas should be almost watery when you finish mashing them. Add to the mashed bananas 1 cup of strained baby food prunes and 1 teaspoon of lemon juice. Mix well with the spoon.
3. Add the whipped cream to the bananas and prunes and mix them together.
4. Cover the bowl with the plate and put into the refrigerator for 1 hour. Then serve at once in the dessert bowls.

Clowns for Dessert *(for 4 people)*

You will need:

1 8-ounce can of sliced
  pineapple (4 slices)
1 pint of vanilla or
  chocolate ice cream
  (1 pint of ice cream
  makes 4 scoops)
4 sugar cones
8 raisins
4 red gumdrops or
  M & M candies
4 small pieces of red
  licorice candy

Use:

Can opener
Sieve
2 bowls
Ice cream scoop
4 small plates

Prepare it this way:

1. Open the can of sliced pineapple. Put the sieve over one bowl. Put the pineapple slices into the sieve. Let the syrup drain off the pineapple slices. Shake the sieve a few times to help the syrup drain off. Put the pineapple slices into the other bowl. Save the syrup to use later in making a gelatin dessert.

2. Set out 4 small plates on the table or work counter. Put 1 pineapple slice on each of the plates.

3. Put 1 scoop of vanilla or chocolate ice cream on top of each pineapple slice. Put the ice cream over the hole in the pineapple slice. The pineapple is the clown's collar.

4. Put 1 ice-cream cone upside down on top of each scoop of ice cream. The cone is the clown's hat.

5. Put 2 raisins in the ice cream a little below the ice-cream cone. The raisins are the clown's eyes. Put a red gumdrop or red M & M candy below and in between the raisins. This is the clown's nose. Put a small piece of red licorice below the nose. This will be the clown's mouth. Eat right away.

AFTER-SCHOOL SNACKS need not be potato chips and Coke. For one things, chips and Coke are bad for your teeth, skin and general health. Not that they don't taste really great sometimes, and not that you must give them up for all time and forever—just don't let them be your *steady* after-school snack treat. A dish of natural cereal, with or without milk, tastes delicious and is a lot better for you than a bag of potato chips. A fruit shake, or a milk shake made with regular skim or powdered milk, is every bit as much of a pick-up as a can of cola. Here are some suggestions for fixing nourishing and healthy after-school snacks for you and your friends. You will find other ideas in cookbooks listed at the end of this book.

Banana Shake (for 2 people)

2 small ripe bananas
1 tablespoon of honey or maple syrup or sugar
2 cups of milk

Put all the ingredients in a blender and mix well for about ½ minute. If you don't have a blender, mash up the bananas well with a fork, add the milk and honey, and stir very well until all blended.

Eggnog (for 2 people)

2 eggs
2 tablespoons of sugar
2 cups of milk
1 teaspoon of vanilla
½ teaspoon of cinnamon

Put all the ingredients in a blender and mix well for about ½ minute. If you don't have a blender, put all the ingredients in a pitcher or bottle with a cover and stir or shake very hard for about 2 or 3 minutes.

Fruit-Juice Shake (for 1 person)

½ cup of cranberry or grape juice
½ cup of orange juice
1 scoop of vanilla ice cream

Put all the ingredients into a blender and mix well for about 1 minute. If you don't have a blender, put all the ingredients in a tall glass and let them stand for about 5 minutes. By that time the ice cream will be soft. Mix well with a long spoon.

Muffin Pizza (for 1 person)

1 English muffin
2 slices of mozzarella cheese
2 tablespoons of tomato sauce or marinara sauce
¼ teaspoon of oregano

Cut the muffin in half. Pour a tablespoon of the tomato sauce over each muffin half. Put a slice of mozzarella cheese on each half. Sprinkle with oregano. Put in the oven, or toaster oven if you have one, at 350°F. for about 10 minutes.

Cottage Cheese Sundae *(for 1 person)*

1 scoop of cottage cheese
¼ cup of raisins or other dried fruit
1 tablespoon of your favorite jam or honey
Nuts or graham cracker crumbs if you have some

Put the scoop of cottage cheese in a bowl. Add the dried fruit and mix well. Put the honey or jam over the cottage cheese. Sprinkle with nuts or graham cracker crumbs. Eat and be healthy.

IF YOU PREPARE LUNCH BOXES for the family, plan the lunch "menu" on the evening before you are to prepare it or on a weekly schedule. If your lunch "menu" includes a canned drink from home, put the can in the refrigerator the evening before you pack it in the lunch box or bag. Nothing tastes as awful as warm fruit juice or fruit drink. If you are to fill thermos bottles with milk or other refrigerated drinks, then you have no such problem.

If you use lunch bags instead of lunch boxes, write on them the names of the family members to whom they will belong the following morning. You can even decorate the bags with a quick drawing done with a felt-tip pen. How about putting a friendly note into your brothers' or sisters' or parents' lunch bags? Everyone likes to be remembered—including parents!

Here are some suggested lunch-box menus for a complete work week. There are cookbooks listed at the end of this book which have many more lunch menus and recipes.

Monday
Leftover-from-the-weekend meat sandwich on
   white bread (sliced meat or chicken salad,
   ham salad, sliced cold meat loaf)
Pickle
Apple, orange or pear
Milk

Tuesday
Peanut butter and raisins sandwich
   on whole wheat bread
Carrot sticks
Cookies
Milk

Wednesday
Egg salad sandwich on rye bread
Celery sticks
Jello in plastic container, or ready-made
    pudding in jar
Milk

Thursday
Tuna salad sandwich on white bread
Radishes
Cookies
Fruit juice

Friday
Triple-decker sandwich with cheddar
    cheese and deviled ham spread
    on dark pumpernickel and white bread
Pickle
Fruit
Milk

6 · Saving Money

Every family has only a certain amount of money to spend—for food, housing, clothing and everything else—and must make decisions about how to spend it. Discuss the family budget with your parents if they are willing. Some parents do not like to discuss their incomes and expenditures with the children in the family. On the other hand, some families like to discuss their budgets with all the members present, so that everyone knows how much is coming in and how much is being spent each month. This permits each family member to know just what the family can afford to do and what must be passed up.

When a budget is discussed, you may want to talk about your allowance—if your family gives you an allowance—in terms of the jobs you perform at home and the total budget. If you feel that your allowance is unfair, speak up! If, on the other hand, your demands are unreasonable within the family's budget, you ought to consider other ways of earning pocket money, such as:

1. Helping out at birthday parties for your neighbors' little children.
2. Baby-sitting for your neighbors.
3. Delivering newspapers.
4. Having a yard sale (or sidewalk sale) of books, and toys you have outgrown.

5. Making and selling lemonade.
6. Shining shoes.
7. Making greeting cards and selling them.
8. Doing errands for an elderly neighbor.
9. Caring for neighbors' pets when they are away.
10. Mowing lawns or shoveling snow.

In addition to earning pocket money, there are many ways in which you can help your family save money. Money saved is often very much like money found, and can sometimes be used for small luxuries. If you have been extra careful about turning off electricity, not using hot water unnecessarily or reducing expenses in other ways, maybe some of the saved money can be used to buy a good paperback book for your library, or a small toy you have been wanting.

SAVE DISCOUNT COUPONS which you may find in your cereal boxes, jars of instant coffee, chocolate powder or wherever else you see them. It is good to keep these coupons in one place—possibly in the same file which you have made for keeping receipts from cleaners, etc. (see page 12). If you put away coupons, they can be easily located when your mom or dad and you go to the supermarket or grocery store.

READ ADVERTISEMENTS in your local paper for food and clothing sales and point them out to your mom or dad. No one expects you to become the greatest bargain-hunter on your block or in your building, but it may be helpful to watch out for sales in your papers or in the windows of your neighborhood stores.

MAKE A LIST OF THINGS YOU MUST BUY if you shop by yourself in the supermarket or grocery store. Do not buy only well-known brands. Compare prices, weights and liquid measurements on everything you buy. An 8-ounce package of noodles from a well-known manufacturer is no better than an 8-ounce package of noodles made by a lesser-known company or one which has the supermarket (house brand) name on it. The same is true of almost everything you may need to buy—so buy the brand which is the least expensive but which equals the name brand in quantity. Be sure to keep an eagle eye out for unadvertised specials on items on your list.

If you buy milk, or other things from the dairy case, look on the cartons for the dates by which these products must be sold. For instance, if the milk carton is marked "November 11" and you are shopping on November 12, don't buy it. The milk may spoil quickly and you will waste your money. Look for a container with a later date. Dates are also printed on loaves of bread and other baked goods, as well as on a number of other fresh and frozen foods. Sometimes, however, day-old baked products are sold at reduced prices—those are certainly worth considering for special purposes. For example, if you need an angel food or chiffon cake for a dessert such as the one described on page 71, a cake that is a day old will do just fine, especially since it will save your family money.

Don't buy things on impulse. If you see popcorn on sale, but it isn't on your shopping list, skip it. Learning to stick to a shopping list and not buy any-

thing extra is a valuable lesson, and money-saving too. But if you have been given permission to spend a little money for a treat, do it and enjoy it.

SAVE UNFINISHED FOOD. For instance, if you have eaten only half an orange, apple or banana, wrap the leftover piece in aluminum foil or other wrapping paper and put it in the refrigerator. You may want to finish it later, or to use it in fruit salad or whatever. If you do use it in fruit salad, be hygienic and carefully cut off the place where you have bitten into the fruit. Save scraps of food for pets—lettuce for your gerbil, meat bits for your dog or cat, etc.

SAVE ELECTRICITY. Turn off all the lights when you leave a room to which you do not intend to come back immediately. Unless you are listening to it, turn off the TV set, the radio or your record player. Many times these machines keep playing without anyone paying any attention to them at all. Electricity is very expensive. Turning off lights, TVs, phonographs, etc. will save your family lots of money. It is also better for our whole economy and environment—saving natural resources is everybody's job!

TURN DOWN THE HEAT if you live in a private house. There is little sense in walking around your home in a short-sleeved polo shirt on a winter day. It's better to put on a sweater or sweat shirt to keep warm than to turn the thermostat above 68 degrees. Lower temperatures in your home are better for your health as well as for your family's budget.

In an apartment it may be harder to regulate the temperature. Some radiators cannot be turned off nor their temperature regulated. If, however, it is possible in your apartment, turn the heat down too. If your landlords save money on their heating oil bills, maybe they will not need to raise your family's rent.

RUN HOT WATER ONLY WHEN NECESSARY. Water is heated by a boiler that runs on electricity, heating oil or gas. All of this costs money. Do not wash and rinse dishes under hot running water. When you wash dishes, close the drain, pour hot water and a little soap liquid or powder into the sink and then wash. After you've finished washing, let the soapy water out, fill the sink with clear water and rinse the dishes.

HELP SAVE GASOLINE. If you live in the country or in the suburbs, keep a list of things you want to do in the nearest town or shopping center and do them on a day when your mom or dad is driving to town. For example, if you need to return or borrow books from your public library, buy art supplies and get a birthday present for a friend, plan to do all of these things on one trip. To make extra trips into the village or shopping center because you have forgotten to buy new pencils or something else guzzles up unnecessary gallons of gasoline in your family's car. Gasoline costs lots of money, so try to help your mom or dad to save it by doing your errands on the same day they do theirs.

USE THE TELEPHONE WISELY. Try to keep telephone conversations with your friends fairly short. There are often extra charges for long telephone calls. To make sure that you do not talk endlessly, it is fun to put an egg timer—if you have one—next to your telephone. When the sand runs out on one end of the egg timer, end the conversation.

Look up telephone numbers in the telephone book. Don't call the telephone operator for non-emergency telephone numbers. In certain communities only three calls for information are free each month. All additional calls for information are now being charged to your family telephone bill. Ask your mom or dad to check on these rules with your local telephone company. But if you need the fire department or the police or the poison control center and you have misplaced their numbers, then call the operator, of course.

WEAR OLD CLOTHES WHEN YOU PLAY or do chores around the house. If you wear good clothes to school, take them off when you return home. Playing or working around the house causes wear and tear on your good clothing, and replacing them costs lots of money. Put on old dungarees, polo shirts and sneakers for playing and working at home.

SAVE AND "RECYCLE" OLD CLOTHING. If you have jeans that are too short or too patched around the knees but still fit you in the waist, cut them off to wear as shorts. If you have single, unmatched socks, you can make hand puppets from them as well as really good furniture- or silver-polishing mitts. Outgrown and torn polo shirts or sweat shirts that can no longer be worn make fine polishing rags, too.

Some schools and community centers have clothing exchange days. If such a program exists in your community, save your outgrown but still wearable clothing for such a day. You may be able to trade the things you cannot wear for things someone else can no longer wear. Possibly your mom or dad gives your outgrown but still wearable clothes to family members and friends with smaller children or to local charitable organizations such as the Salvation Army, Goodwill Industries or thrift shops run by hospitals and other organizations.

HELP WITH MINOR REPAIRS AND MENDING.

You can help your mom or dad paint the kitchen cabinets or even entire rooms in your home. Watch how your mom or dad paints and then learn to paint the woodwork or closet doors or parts of walls by yourself.

Learn how to sew up hems on your pants or dresses, sew on buttons or mend ripped seams.

Learn how to use simple tools such as a hammer, screwdriver, wrench, etc. There are some simply written house repair books in your library (see the list at the end of this book). If you are interested in such information, borrow some and look them over. Then when repairs are needed around your home, you can be useful in helping your mom or dad.

START A VEGETABLE GARDEN.

If you live in the suburbs or in the country and have a big enough yard, ask your parents to help you plant your own vegetables. There are many books for young people, and adults as well, on starting a vegetable garden. Borrow some from your library, or buy a paperback or two on gardening (see the list of gardening books at the end of this book). Read them with your mom or dad and start a garden in your yard.

If you have sufficient sunlight in your apartment, you can start an indoor herb garden and even grow tomato plants. Borrow books on indoor gardening and find out how to get started. Fresh herbs and vegetables taste better than store-bought ones and they save money for your family as well.

Tending an indoor or an outdoor garden is a lot of fun and can keep you happily busy for many hours, especially during summer vacation. If you have an outdoor garden, you may want to start a small compost pile to use as natural fertilizer for the soil. Save vegetable peelings, coffee grounds, etc. in a separate plastic garbage bag. Add them to your compost pile each evening.

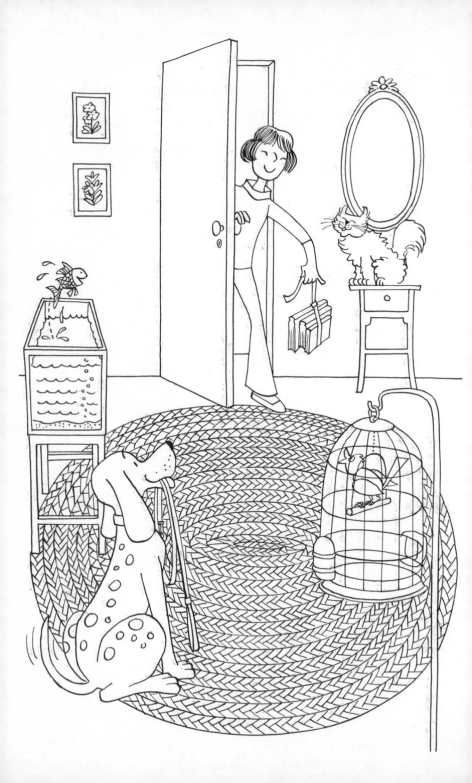

7 · Caring for Pets

If you have pets in your home—a dog or a cat, a canary or goldfish—decide who takes care of which pet on which days. Unless you all know who feeds whom, and when, you will have either a very fat or very hungry pet. (Goldfish have been known to perish as much from over-feeding as from hunger!)

IF YOU HAVE A DOG, and are the only child in the family old enough to walk it or the only child at home while your parents work, then you may be responsible for walking the dog as soon as you come home from school. Never let your dog run without a leash—not in the city, not in the country, not in the suburbs. Too many accidents happen when a dog is off the leash and free to run and chase. If you walk your dog in the city, get the dog off the sidewalk to do his business. Choose a less busy side street to walk your dog; do not walk on a heavily traveled avenue. Walk as close to the curb as you can, and hold your dog's leash tightly in your hand. After the dog has finished, walk him around for exercise. Put fresh water in the dog's dish when you come home, and if it is your duty, feed it between 4:00 and 5:00 P.M.

IF YOU HAVE A CAT, clean out the litter box as soon as you come home from school. The place where the litter box stands sometimes may have an odor, so spray with deodorant all around the room. If it is your job to change the kitty litter in the box, do the following: Throw the dirty litter in the trash. Wash the box with soap and water and a little baking soda. After you put fresh litter in the box, add ½ cup of baking soda to it. The baking soda takes away some of the odor. Give the cat fresh water, and feed it the food it is used to getting at the usual time.

IF YOU HAVE OTHER PETS—such as gerbils, mice, hamsters, birds or fish—you will need to feed them and clean their cage and/or tank. Cage or tank cleaning, of course, need not be done before your parents come home from work. You can do it at whatever time has been put aside for it in your family's weekly schedule of chores.

IF YOUR PET HAS HAD AN ACCIDENT ON THE RUG, take your pet back to the spot and scold it severely for its bad behavior. If the "mess" can be picked up and flushed down the toilet, pick it up with lots of toilet paper and throw it out. If the "mess" is a puddle, mop it up with many pieces of paper towel or a rag. Throw the rag or paper towels in the trash.

When you have removed as much as possible of the "mess," do the following. Mix 2 cups of lukewarm water with ½ cup of white vinegar and a little soap powder or liquid. Soak a sponge or rag in the water-vinegar-soap mixture. Wring it out and rub the spot on which your pet has had an accident. Repeat this several times. Throw out the rag or sponge. This should remove the stain and discourage your pet from having future accidents in the same place.

IF YOU DO NOT HAVE ANY PETS at all and wish you had one to keep you company while your parents are at work, it may be a good idea to read some books on caring for and training various pets. Borrow books from your library, or get some paperbacks on this subject (see the list of titles at the end of this book). Find out about the care various pets require. Decide, with your parents' help, whether there is a pet that would fit in with your household and for which you could assume major responsibility. If your parents feel confident that the pet you have chosen will not be an added burden on the family's busy schedule, perhaps they will agree to let you have it. If so, get it and enjoy taking care of it.

8 · Baby-Sitting With Brothers and Sisters

If you baby-sit for your younger brothers or sisters, treat the assignment as you would treat a paying job. In some families, though by no means all of them, older brothers and sisters receive a token fee for baby-sitting for younger brothers and sisters. This may be especially true if you were offered a paid baby-sitting job elsewhere for the same period of time. Make an agreement with your parents as to how this will work in your family—whether baby-sitting will be a separate, paid assignment or a regular part of your family duties.

Some of your younger brothers and sisters may attend a day-care center while you are in school, they may go to a day-care center after school or they may be picked up by an adult baby-sitter after school. Other arrangements may also have been made for them which do not involve you. However, if you do baby-sit for your brothers and/or sisters, be prepared for the job and find ways to make it enjoyable for everyone in the family.

Get a good baby-sitter's guide book from the library, or in paperback from your local book shop. There are several good books on this subject (see the list at the end of this book). In the meantime, here are some suggestions for you.

SAFETY RULES FOR BABY-SITTERS. All safety measures which apply to your own well-being apply also when you baby-sit (read Chapter 2 on safety measures).

Keep all emergency numbers where you can find them quickly. Just to repeat the numbers you will need to have:

1. Your mom's and/or dad's telephone numbers at work.
2. Your doctor's office and home telephone numbers.
3. The police department's number.
4. The fire department's number.
5. A close friend's or neighbor's number.
6. Poison control center's number in your own or a nearby town (there are over six hundred of them across the country).

The instructions which follow give advice on how to deal with the most commonly occurring ailments or accidents. They should be memorized by you and also hung on a bulletin board or other prominent place in your home.

Be sure there is a simple book on first aid and a first-aid kit in your home and that you know where they are. You can buy a first-aid kit in the dime store or make your own from an empty shoe box. It is easier to find first-aid equipment if it is kept in a separate place, not in your bathroom medicine cabinet. The first-aid kit should include Band-Aids, sterile gauze pads, tape, rubbing alcohol, Mercurochrome, an eye-cup, petroleum jelly, an ointment to soothe minor burns and scratches and whatever else your parents decide on.

If your brother or sister has a mild headache or stomachache, make him or her lie down. If the weather is chilly, cover her or him with a blanket. Call one of your parents to report and to ask for advice. Never give or take any medicines without first checking with your mom or dad. *Never, never, never!*

In case of a nosebleed, make the child sit quietly, with a towel to catch the blood. Take a few ice cubes from the freezer and wrap them in a towel or put them in a plastic bag. Put the ice on the back of the child's neck or the forehead. This should stop the bleeding. If, after about five minutes, it doesn't, call one of your parents.

In case of a broken bone, don't move the child around or give anything to eat or drink. Cover him or her with a blanket, and telephone your parents and the police. The police will take the child to the nearest hospital and they will discuss the situation with one of your parents.

In case of cuts and scrapes, wash the wound with cool water and put on some Mercurochrome or ointment from your first-aid kit. Put a gauze pad or Band-Aid over it. If the bleeding from the scrape or cut does not stop, call one of your parents and ask for further directions.

A bruise will heal more quickly if you apply ice cubes wrapped in a towel or plastic bag.

In case of a minor skin burn, apply petroleum jelly or vegetable shortening or, if you have it in your first-aid kit, an ointment intended for minor burns. Another method of treating a minor burn is to run cold water on the burned area or apply ice cubes. If a blister develops, do not break it. Cover it loosely with a sterile gauze pad and tape. If it is anything more than a tiny, minor burn, call the police and one of your parents *immediately;* even if it is a tiny, minor burn, call one of your parents and describe to him or her what happened and how you have handled the situation.

Dust in the eye can be removed in several ways. Take hold of the upper lashes and move the upper eyelid down and away from the eye. This will make the eye tear and help the dust to come out. If it doesn't and you have an eyecup in your first-aid kit, fill it with clear, cool water. Make the child lower his or her head and put the eye over the water-filled eyecup. Then have the child raise the head, holding the cup against the eye, and tell him or her to blink rapidly a few times. If you do not have an eyecup, squeeze water into the eye from a clean washcloth or sponge. The water should wash out the dust. If the child still complains of something in his or her eye, call one of your parents right away. It is possible that the dust, or other speck, settled on the eyeball and may need to be removed by a doctor. Do not allow the child to rub his or her eye.

If the child is choking, turn him or her upside-down or make the child lean over a chair and smack him or her very hard between the shoulder blades. Whatever was choking the child should come out of the windpipe. Call the police and one of your parents right away if this does not help immediately.

If you think the child has swallowed poison, call a poison control center immediately. Such centers are located all over the country, and if there isn't one in your home town, there surely will be one in a nearby town or city. However, if you cannot reach one, call your doctor and one of your parents right away. Try to identify to the poison control center, or to your doctor, the poison which you think the child has swallowed. Nearby bottles or containers should give you clues. Smelling the child's clothing or mouth may help. Look for burns on lips and mouth. Describe your findings to the poison control center or to your doctor. If you do not know what the poison is, describe as best as you can the child's symptoms, such as stomach cramps, sleepiness, nausea, etc. Follow instructions given to you over the telephone. If you have not been able to reach the poison control center or your doctor, call the police, tell them what happened and ask for immediate help.

All this sounds pretty scary and complicated, and it can be if you aren't prepared to cope with such a situation. However, if you do know how to cope, you will be able to handle it very well indeed.

ADDITIONAL SAFETY TIPS. If you go out with young brothers or sisters, always hold their hands on the street, especially if they are less than five years old. Little kids have a habit of running ahead or dawdling behind, which may make a nervous wreck of you even before you become a parent!

Do not let little children play with plastic bags, sharp objects or matches. Never let them play near a stove, near an open window, by a stairway or near an electrical outlet. Never let them touch electrical outlets with their hands or with their toys. Make sure that they play only with large objects, like toys or pots and pans from your kitchen. Do not let them play with teeny-tiny objects which they can put into their mouths and possibly swallow. Do not let them near closets where cleaning supplies are kept, nor anywhere near the medicine cabinet. Do not leave them alone in the house or apartment, not even for a minute.

HOW TO AMUSE YOUNG CHILDREN. With your parents' help, prepare a box with "craft equipment" which you can use with younger brothers and sisters (this will be handy for you as well). Such an equipment box should include colored construction paper, old magazines, blunt scissors, white glue, colored masking tape, a hole-punch, crayons, scraps of lace and other fabrics, modeling clay, poster paints, extra shoelaces and whatever else you can round up for craft projects. If you are properly equipped for times when you have to baby-sit, hours will go by faster and more happily for everyone, and especially for you.

Take out books from the library which you can read to your younger brothers and sisters. A nice long story hour with younger children is fun for them and for you, too. As you practice your storytelling and acting talents, your reading skills will also improve. Help the children act out characters from their favorite nursery rhymes or books. Suggest that they pretend to be a tree swaying in the wind, or an airplane taking off from an airport, or anything else you can dream up. Ask them what they would like you to act out. This game of play-acting and pretending can go on for some time and be pleasurable for everyone.

There are many craft books with simple projects which you can make with your younger sisters or brothers (see the list at the end of this book). When you have no craft books handy, you might try the following projects. They are simple and quick and need no fancy equipment or materials.

Grocery Bag Masks

You will need: two large brown grocery-store bags; scissors; red and black felt-tip pens.

Do it this way:
1. Cut out slits for the eyes and mouth on each of the bags.
2. With black felt-tip pen, draw eyelashes around the slits for the eyes.

3. With black felt-tip pen, draw a large and bushy mustache over the slit for the mouth. Below the slit for the mouth draw the biggest and bushiest beard you can.

4. Draw lips over the slit for the mouth with red felt-tip pen. The second mask can be similar to the first or completely different—without a mustache and beard but with red cheeks and black hair drawn in a helter-skelter fashion, for example.

Decorated Shopping Bags

You will need: brown shopping bags from the supermarket; felt-tip pens or colorful paper scraps; glue; newspapers.

Do it this way:

1. Help your younger brother or sister to draw with felt-tip pens the wildest designs he or she wishes all over the brown bags. Or glue scraps of colorful paper in a wild pattern all over the bags. If you use glue, spread newspapers on your working space.

2. The same can be done on brown lunch bags for the family. They will be nice and cheerful!

Stained-Glass Window Picture

You will need: newspapers; 1 piece of colored construction paper; scraps of colored cellophane from candy wrappers; scissors; glue or Scotch tape; 1 shoelace.

Do it this way:

1. Spread newspapers on your working area. Cut out variously shaped holes in the sheet of construction paper.
2. Paste or tape scraps of cellophane paper over the holes.
3. Make a hole on the top of the piece of paper. Pull the shoelace through the hole. Hang in a sunny window.

Lacy Place Mats

You will need: newspapers; 8 pieces of differently colored construction paper; scissors; glue.

Do it this way:

1. Spread newspapers on your working area. Fold 4 pieces of construction paper in half and then in half again. Cut out different shapes from each of the edges of the folded papers.
2. Unfold the papers which you have cut. They will have unexpected designs.
3. Glue these lacy-design pieces of paper over the other, un-cut, pieces of construction paper. The differently colored, un-cut construction papers will peek through the holes and look nice. These can be used as place mats for a special family meal, or as presents.

9 · Parents Who Work at Home

If one or both of your parents work at home, it is very hard for you not to barge in on them whenever you want. Some parents may not mind being interrupted at their work, but others most certainly do. If your father happens to be a musician and he is practicing a particularly difficult passage, an interruption can destroy many minutes of concentrated effort. If your mother happens to be a writer and is concentrating on her work, an interruption for some unimportant question, such as "Where is my blue shirt?" when you can easily wear the yellow one or find the blue one yourself, can also be annoying and disruptive.

Of course, if there is a real emergency of some kind, your mom or dad will want to know, but a lot of unimportant questions make it impossible for him or her to work. The advantage of having parents who work at home is the knowledge that they are always there when you really, truly need them. It may be hard at times, though, not to demand their attention for whatever pops into your mind. Discuss with your "at-home-but-working" parent when you can and when you must not interrupt her or him. Perhaps you can set up some signal—three knocks on the door?—that your needs are urgent. Even if your mom's or dad's desk or worktable is in the bedroom or in a corner of the living room or the middle of the kitchen, try to respect the fact that they are working and need to concentrate.

If you feel that it is truly beyond your endurance to be in the same house with them for hours at a time and not be able to talk to them, then tell them so. Perhaps when your mom or dad takes a break from work, you can sit with him or her for a few uninterrupted minutes and have a chat and/or snack.

HELPFUL THINGS YOU CAN DO for your mom or dad who works at home. You can answer the telephone and take messages without disturbing him or her. You might say "My mom is working now, but she will call you back." You might sharpen pencils, empty the wastepaper baskets or make a cup of tea or coffee for him or her. How about a funny sign for the desk or working space or door? "Hush, Genius at Work" or "Psst, Dad Is Practicing Beethoven" (or Scott Joplin, or any other composer you yourself enjoy) or "Silence, Mom Is Designing the Next Empire State Building" or whatever.

WHEN YOU HAVE AFTER-SCHOOL VISITORS, you might explain your particular situation to your friends. Sometimes it may be hard for you not to play noisily near or in the room where your parent works. But if your parent's work requires concentration and not too much noise, you might as well explain it to your pals ahead of time.

On the other hand, there are advantages to this situation, too! For example, if your friend takes piano lessons and your dad or mom is a professional musician, it may be fun for the three of you to talk about music for a few minutes. Your mom or dad may even want to show your friend how he or she practices, or to time Chopin's "Minute Valse" and see if it really can be played in only one minute. If your parent is a professional dressmaker, and your friend is interested in sewing, maybe they can discuss their interests together.

Ask your mom or dad to try to arrange the afternoon so that you and your friend can spend a few minutes with her or him—if that is what you would like to do. Talking things over, and planning them ahead of time, always makes life easier for everyone in a family.

10 · Absent Parents

If your parent's job requires a lot of travel, you may sometimes feel resentful, frustrated and unhappy, especially if that parent is not at home to share in your birthday celebrations, or to attend an important sports event in school, or to be present at a school concert. The same may be true if your parents are divorced or separated and one of them lives so far away that you do not see him or her very often. Discuss these feelings with your parents and bring them out into the open. Life will be much easier for all of you if you express your feelings honestly.

Try to remember that it is every bit as hard for your mother or father to miss some of the important events in your life. It is not that he or she wants to be away from you. Sometimes it is simply the way life has turned out to be. Some professions and jobs do require a lot of traveling. Musicians, salespeople, actors, members of the armed forces must be away from their homes for short and long periods of time, and that is that. Since you cannot change the situation, try to learn to live with it as comfortably as you can. Do whatever possible to make life happier for yourself and for your absent parent.

Here are some ideas to help you keep a feeling of closeness when you are away from each other.

ASK QUESTIONS ABOUT PLACES your parent will be seeing while traveling on business or where he or she lives. Read about these places with your parent, or by yourself. This will help you to "see" what your parent will be seeing and where he or she is staying.

ASK FOR POSTCARDS AND FOLDERS. If you can receive mail in school, ask your parent to send you lots of postcards or folders in care of your teacher. If you want to, you can then share these interesting cards or folders from far or nearby places with your teacher and classmates. These may be especially interesting when you study geography, or social studies, or map-making, or history.

WRITE FREQUENT LETTERS even if they are not long ones. Postcards, mailed almost daily, are just as good for keeping in touch with your mom or dad and help you share what is happening in your life.

SEND PHOTOGRAPHS FREQUENTLY and, if possible, ask for the same from your absent parent. Ask your at-home parent, baby-sitter, brother, sister or friend to take pictures of you. You can also go into the dime store and take pictures of yourself in a photograph booth. Draw pictures of yourself, or your pets, or anything else you like, and send them on as well.

KEEP A NOTEBOOK. Write down in it some of the important events which have occurred while you and your dad or mom were away from each other. Later, when you see your parent again, you can share this notebook and talk about all the things that happened.

MAKE TAPES for your absent parent if you have a cassette tape recorder. Tell about some of the exciting events which have occurred. You can share these experiences by sending the tapes to him or her or listening to them with your parent when you are together again.

IF YOUR PARENT IS ABSENT FOR A VERY LONG TIME, you may want to make a mark on a door, or on a long piece of paper, to show how tall you were when you were last together. When you and your parent are reunited, you can check to see how much you grew. Go over your school books and notebooks with your parent before he or she leaves and after you get together once more. Your parent will be able to see just what you have studied and learned while you were apart.

11 · When the Work Is Done

After the housework and the food shopping are finished and all the other chores have been accomplished, there is always time left for family fun. Discuss with your parents what you all would like to do as a family. Of course, there will be times when your mom or dad needs time to be alone, each one by himself or herself, or with each other or with friends. At times like these, you might as well do things with your friends, your grandparents or other relatives. But when you can do things together as a family, there are many interesting plans to be made and followed through.

Find a hobby that your whole family can participate in. It could be rock climbing, skating, hiking, stamp collecting or anything that all of you like to do.

Write to the local chamber of commerce or visitor's bureau, as a surprise to your mom or dad. Ask for free booklets of places to see and things to do in your area. Find out what is happening in your local schools, parks or museums. Often there are concerts and exhibits given completely free of charge. In addition to big museums, you may be able to visit lesser known places of interest. Perhaps a President lived in your area years ago? Or a famous artist, musician or writer? Sometimes beautifully restored old homes are open to the public free or for a small fee. Ask your chamber of commerce to send you information about places of historical interest nearby. An extra bonus will be getting your own mail!

When your parents entertain family, neighbors or close friends, get involved in the preparations for the party. There is so much you can do to help that will be fun for you, too.

In a family where all the work is shared equally, the fun and good times shared together are enormously satisfying and enjoyable.

For Additional Reading

The books suggested in this section are merely examples of the many titles which are available from your library or bookstore. If you cannot find the titles listed below, ask your librarian or bookseller for advice and suggestions. He or she will be able to recommend other books which are equally helpful and interesting.

Books for Baby-Sitters

American National Red Cross, The. *Standard First Aid and Personal Safety*. The American National Red Cross (paperback).

Bendick, Jeanne. *The Emergency Book*. Rand Mc-

Sherman, Sharon. *Baby-Sitter's Guide*. Starline Books (paperback).

Spock, Benjamin C. *Baby and Child Care*. Pocket Books (paperback).

Books on Making and Handling Money

Amazing Life Games Co., The. *Good Cents: Every Kid's Guide to Making Money*. Houghton Mifflin (paperback).

Lee, Mary P. *Money and Kids: How to Earn It, Save It, and Spend It*. Westminster (paperback).

Craft Books

Beech, Linda. *Things to Make and Do.* Starline Books (paperback).

Choate, Judith, and Green, Jane. *Scrapcraft: 50 Easy-to-Make Handicrafts Projects.* Doubleday.

Cobb, Vicki. *Arts and Crafts You Can Eat.* Lippincott (paperback).

Gilbreath, Alice. *Fun and Easy Things to Make.* Starline Books (paperback).

Hautzig, Esther. *Let's Make More Presents: Easy and Inexpensive Gifts for Every Occasion.* Macmillan.

———. *Let's Make Presents: One Hundred Gifts for Less Than One Dollar.* Crowell.

Klimo, Joan F. *What Can I Do Today? A Treasury of Crafts for Children.* Pantheon (paperback).

Lewis, Shari. *Making Easy Puppets.* Dutton.

Lynch, John. *How to Make Mobiles.* Viking (paperback).

Peake, Miriam. *One Hundred and One Things to Make for Fun or Money.* Starline Books (paperback).

Rockwell, Harlow. *I Did It.* Macmillan.

———. *Printmaking.* Doubleday.

Seidelman, James E., and Mintonye, Grace. *Creating with Paper.* Collier (paperback).

———. *Shopping Cart Art.* Macmillan.

Zarchy, Harry. *Creative Hobbies.* Knopf.

Cookbooks

Beebe, Ann. *Easy Cooking: Simple Recipes for Beginning Cooks.* Morrow.

Better Homes and Gardens Books, ed. *Better Homes and Gardens Junior Cook Book*. Meredith.

Cooper, Terry T., and Ratner, Marilyn. *Many Hands Cooking: An International Cookbook for Girls and Boys*. Crowell.

Farmer, Fannie. *Fannie Farmer Junior Cook Book*. Bantam (paperback).

Girl Scouts of the USA. *The Beginner's Cookbook*. Dell (paperback).

Hautzig, Esther. *Cool Cooking: 16 Recipes Without a Stove*. Lothrop, Lee & Shepard.

Knopf, Mildred O. *Around America: A Cookbook for Young People*. Knopf.

McDonald, Barbara. *Casserole Cooking Fun*. Walck (paperback).

Perl, Lila. *The Hamburger Book: All About Hamburgers and Hamburger Cookery*. Seabury.

Pinkwater, Jill. *The Natural Snack Cookbook*. Four Winds.

Seranne, Ann. *America Cooks*. Berkley (paperback).

Stubis, Patricia. *Sandwichery: Riddles, Recipes and Funny Facts About Food*. Parents Magazine Press.

Gardening Books

Brown, Louise Bush. *Young America's Garden Book*. Scribner.

Cutler, Katherine. *Growing a Garden Indoors or Out*. Morrow.

Eckstein, Joan, and Gleit, Joyce. *Fun With Growing Things*. Avon (paperback).

Mandry, Kathy. *How to Grow a Jelly Glass Farm.* Pantheon.

Paul, Aileen. *Kids Gardening.* Doubleday.

——. *Kids Indoor Gardening.* Archway (paperback).

Sholinsky, Jane. *Growing Plants from Fruits and Vegetables.* Starline Books (paperback).

House Repair Books

Boy Scouts of America. *Home Repairs.* Boy Scouts of America.

Nunn, Richard. *Emergency Home Repairs.* Oxmoor House (paperback). This is a book for adults which may prove useful for young readers, too.

Pet Books

Chrystie, Frances. *Pets.* Little, Brown.

Hess, Lilo, and Hogner, Dorothy C. *Odd Pets.* Crowell.

Morgan, Alfred. *Pet Book for Boys and Girls.* Scribner.

Shuttlesworth, Dorothy E. *Pets and People.* Dutton.

——. *Caring for Gerbils and Other Small Pets.* Starline Books (paperback).

Stevens, Carla, and Weil, Lisl. *Your First Pet.* Macmillan.

Index

119

122 HOW TO LIVE WITH WORKING PARENTS

Menus: dinner, 49–50; lunch-box, 78–79; weekend lunch, 50

Message Box, Telephone, 13

Messages, telephone, how to take, 23

Milk stains, how to clean, 32–33

Mint Pudding, Chocolate, 68–69

Mixer, electric, how to use, 42–43

Money: how to save, 81–89; for phone calls, 15; ways of earning, 81–82

Mops, using, 31

Muffin Pizza, 76–77

Musical Comb, 9

Neatness, 29–31

Newspapers: crafts using, 102–103; discarding, 30

Nosebleed, first aid for, 97

Notebook for absent parents, 110–111

Paper bags, crafts using, 101–102

Parents: absent from home, 109–111; working at home, 105–107

Parents' jobs, learning about, 5–6

Pets, care of, 91–93

Photographs, to and from absent parents, 110

Picture Puzzles, 10

Picture, Stained-Glass Window, 102–103

Pictures, Three-Dimensional, 8–9

Pineapple and Ham Salad, 57–58

Pizza, Muffin, 76–77

Place Mats, Lacy, 103

Plants, care of, 34–35

Plastic utensils, in dishwasher, 41

Poem, writing a joint, 9–10

Poison control centers, 24, 99

Poisoning, symptoms of, 99

Police alarm box, 15, 18

Postcards, to and from absent parents, 110

Potato chips, 75

Potatoes and Fish Fillets in Cream Sauce, 63–64

Prices of food, comparing, 83

Projects: for family fun, 113–114; joint poem or story, 9–10; musical comb, 9; personal diary, 11; sorting and filing sports cards, 11–12. See also Crafts

Prune-Banana Whip, 73

Pudding, Chocolate Mint, 68–69

Puzzles, Picture, 10

Railroad tracks, crossing, 16

Receipts, cleaner's, etc., file-folder for, 12

Recipes

APPETIZERS
Fruit Cocktail, 52–53; Grapefruit Cups with Honey, 51–52

DESSERTS
Apple Cake, 71–72; Apple-sauce with Sour Cream, 71; Banana-Prune Whip, 73; Chocolate Cookies in Cream, 67–68; Chocolate Mint Pudding, 68–69;

Clowns, 74–75; Cranberry Whip, 69–71

DRINKS. *See* Shakes

MAIN COURSES
Egg, Corn and Cheese Puff, 60–62; Fish Fillets and Potatoes in Cream Sauce, 63–64; Fried Ham and Cheese Sandwiches, 62–63; Ham and Pineapple Salad, 57–58; Meatball and Rice Casserole, 65–67; Salmon Salad, 58–60; Sweet and Sour Chicken with Rice, 64–65

SALADS
Ham and Pineapple, 57–58; Salmon, 58–60

SHAKES
Banana, 75; Eggnog, 76; Fruit-Juice, 76

SNACKS
Cottage Cheese Sundae, 77; Muffin Pizza, 76–77

SOUPS
Chilled Cream of Chicken, 55–56; Gazpacho, 53–54; Tomato-Sour Cream, 54–55

Recipes, using, 48

Repairs, minor, 88

Rice and Meatball Casserole, 65–67

Rice, Sweet and Sour Chicken with, 64–65

Rugs: removing gum from, 33; removing stains from, 32–33

Safety rules: for baby-sitters, 96–100; general, 15–27

Sales, food and clothing, 82

Sal soda, for removing stains, 32–33

Sandwiches: for lunch boxes, 78–79; Fried Ham and Cheese, 62–63

Saving money, 81–89

Scrapes, first aid for, 97

Shopping Bags, Decorated, 102

Showers, taking, 24–25

Sickness, what to do in case of, 25. *See also* First aid tips for baby-sitters

Soap powder, to use, 39

Socks, washing, 39–40

Soft-drink stains, 32–33

Sour Cream, Applesauce with, 71

Sour Cream-Tomato Soup, 54–55

Spanish Soup (Gazpacho), 53–54

Sports cards, file for, 11–12

Spots. *See* Stains

Stained-Glass Window Picture, 102–103

Stains, how to clean, 32–33, 92–93

Stomachache, first aid for, 97

Story, writing a joint, 9–10

Storytelling, 101

Strangers: being followed by, 20; dealing with, on street, 17; ringing doorbells, 22; on the telephone, 23

Streets: being followed on, 17, 20; crossing, 16; if attacked on, 17–18; playing near, 16; walking on, 16–17, 20

Subway, riding, 15–16

Sundae, Cottage Cheese, 77

Sweet and Sour Chicken with Rice, 64–65